Outrageous Behavior-Mod

Handbook of Strategic Interventions
For Managing Impossible Students

PRO-ED, Inc.

Copyright © 1997

Disclaimer

PERSONAL NOTE TO THE READER: The unorthodox methods presented in this handbook are offered for instructional and educational purposes only. OBM interventions have been developed by eccentric school psychology practitioners and should be applied only after due consideration---and at your own risk! Please be aware that the actual use of these nonstandard techniques may result in temporary confusion and disorientation for your oppositional-defiant students. Also be aware that some child-centered educators have expressed concern that OBM methods may cause disruptive students to act civil and complete assignments *against their will.* OBM users must assume all responsibility for their successes!

Acknowledgments

The present handbook represents a small step in the journey toward strategic classroom management. The author openly admits to compiling and systematizing the methods, but many outstanding school psychologists and classroom instructors must also share blame and recognition for their co-conspiracy. From the early days of experimentation in the field, Phyllis Crawford, M.A., Cliff Jones, Ph.D., Barbara Fishgrab, M.A. (wannabee Ph.D.), and Frank Amadeo, M.A. (no-needa Ph.D.), have critiqued, insulted, and generally encouraged the development of the strategies presented in this handbook.

This intrepid cadre of counselors has provided effective psychological service to the Gallup-McKinley County Schools (New Mexico), one of the largest geographic school districts in North America. This group was one of those rare counseling staffs that could pull together like a MASH team for crisis intervention, or work independently as unseen Lone Rangers in far flung desert schools. These professionals have taught me more in our "outrageous" staff consults and through their counseling successes than I have ever imparted to them. Thanks guys!

Finally, the author is indebted to hundreds of teachers, administrators, and guidance counselors who have attended his inservice training workshops across New Mexico and Arizona. These classroom practitioners have helped to refine the various wacky interventions and keep them almost grounded in reality. For the behavior management work you do everyday in our schools, this OBM Handbook is also dedicated to you!

Barry T. Christian, Ph.D.
Clinical Psychologist
Supervising School Psychologist

Graphics: Besides many items lifted from *Corel Draw!*, you will find some interesting student-generated illustrations. Special thanks to Chad Scarbro and Erika Christian for sharing their talents.

Table of Contents

Chapter One

Introduction To Strategic Management

What's So "Outrageous" About It?

Many of the methods presented in this handbook are "strategic" in nature. That is, they tend to avoid direct power confrontations with resistant students, and instead use pre-planned interactions which confuse and erode the difficult behaviors. These strategic methods include not only the learning principles of more traditional behavior modification, but also many hypnotic methods and psycholinguistic principles that address the student's resistance at a deeper "personality level". Over the years of teacher consultation, workshop training programs,

and real world practice, this rather unorthodox approach has come to be affectionately known as "Outrageous B-Mod", or simply "OBM" for those savvy folks on the inside.

Some OBM methods make use of planned confusion or disruptive word pictures. Others may incorporate double bind requests and off beat "psycho-babble" interpretations. Among our favorite are the straight-faced paradoxic assignments that appear to encourage the problem behaviors---while gently disrupting and fogging them. The real beauty of OBM methods is that they skillfully make use of the student's own stubbornness and rigid style to fuel the desired changes. We've sometimes described it as "programmatic judo" since the resistance energy is strategically used to defeat the misbehavior. Therefore, the more oppositional a student is, the better these methods seem to work. Hey, what a deal!

Lt. Columbo in the Classroom

We have found that OBM methods are partly an arsenal of outlandish strategies and partly a playful engaging attitude. It has also become apparent that this approach is geared more to micro-management situations in the classroom (i.e., those predictable face-to-face power struggles), rather than toward district level behavior policies. OBM interventions are not intended to replace the foundational management principles by which most of the daily classroom routine is organized. Rather, our proposed methods are for those critical situations where power-thirsty students "reflexively" defy limits and boldly go where no students have gone before in usurping authority.

Although nearly every teacher, administrator, or counselor can make some use of OBM methods, we have found that certain folks are the "naturals". These gifted educators have the innate capacity to simultaneously follow an OBM workshop lecture and also drift away in their own private thought world to plan a half dozen creative interventions. Some teacher trainees have been heard to suddenly laugh out loud during a workshop ---and then snap out of their trance with some grinning embarrassment. Having read only the first few lines of our handbook, you may already have an idea whether OBM is for you. We hope it is!

Depending on your own personality style, closeness to retirement, and medication level, you may find yourself strangely amused with the possibilities of OBM...or not. As you move further into the handbook, keep in mind that many of the classroom interventions have multiple levels of meaning.

Consider the way Lt. Columbo interrogates his prime suspects. One observer may see a bumbling detective wandering about in a rumpled trench coat. This inept guy seems to be a sorry excuse for a detective. He misses obvious clues, gets distracted with trivial conversation, and seems to misinterpret the key facts. Of course the rest of us look on with little worry for the gifted detective. To us, his subtle interviews are like a 3-D chess game and may rank as a classic art form. The unassuming questions crafted by this sleuth reveal a quietly competent genius going about his life's work.

Hopefully, you'll discover some of the same Lt. Columbo artistry in this strategic approach to behavior management. At this point, keep in mind that any tokens, charts, or rewards included in our classroom methods are only "props" and not the real substance. Welcome to the emerging technology of Outrageous B-Mod!

Who Are These Oppositional-Defiant Students?

In case you didn't catch it the first time around, let us say it one---more---time: The classroom interventions presented in this handbook are not offered for "general" classroom management. It will become obvious that these specialized OBM methods are best suited for a type of student we call "Oppositional-Defiant". In fact the psychiatric community has also included this same category as a "Disorder of Childhood or Adolescence" in their DSM-IV diagnostic code book. The shrinks have recognized this type of kid for years...but classroom teachers have known them since Aristotle opened his first think tank. It is interesting that this particular category is distinguished from dozens of other conduct, emotional, and developmental disorders. In general, these difficult young people are easily identified by their inordinate thirst for power and conquest. They are wired to question authority and lust after control. It seems that they come to us preprogrammed at the factory to resist any limits placed upon them.

One conclusion we might draw from the above list of traits is that these are "kids with an attitude". They may not be mugging little old ladies or struggling with deep depression, but they do have a commanding "presence" in any classroom. Sooner or later they will come into conflict with the established hierarchy of authority. Too bad if you happen to represent that authority.

Sound like some students you've met? Keep in mind that they are not necessarily gang members or juvenile offenders (although they can be). They are not necessarily emotionally disturbed (although they can be). And they are not necessarily Attention Deficit kids (although, Heaven help us, they can be). Let's think for a second about one of your most impossible students. Mentally insert his name in the following form and consider each of the diagnostic criteria. Maybe you have a certifiable case on your hands?

Oppositional-Defiant Disorder

My Student: _____

Certifiable Banana? _____ Yes _____ No _____ Most Likely

The American Psychiatric Association's DSM-IV diagnostic criteria for Oppositional Defiant Disorder indicates that these children show a long term pattern of negativistic, hostile, and defiant behaviors that include at least *four* of the following traits:

 ____ 1. **Often loses temper**
 ____ 2. **Often argues with adults**
 ____ 3. **Often actively defies or refuses to comply with adults' requests or rules**
 ____ 4. **Often deliberately annoys people**
 ____ 5. **Often blames others for his or her mistakes or misbehavior**
 ____ 6. **Is often touchy or easily annoyed by others**
 ____ 7. **Is often angry and resentful**
 ____ 8. **Is often spiteful or vindictive**

The Lighter Side of Classroom Tyrants

Since my uncommon staff of school psychology counselors will never let well-enough alone, we have moved beyond the DSM-IV diagnosis with some real world descriptors of our own. Below are a few of the criterion traits that suggest you may have an Oppositional-Defiant student in your class:

1. While completing a career preference worksheet, he asks you for the proper spelling of "despot".
2. In explaining today's playground altercation, he confidently asserts that the other students forced his wrath---because they were too slow in obeying his commands.
3. He is able to methodically list dozens of exception clauses to each of your class rules. Given an opportunity, he can also do a convincing F. Lee Baily defense of any infraction.
4. You find yourself *not* making reasonable requests of him, just to avoid that whining song and dance.
5. You award one of the nicest prizes ever given to a student....and he looks up to ask "Is this all?"
6. You learn he was the only guest ever asked to leave *Mr. Roger's Neighborhood.*
7. You receive a curt, business-like memo from this student informing you that his Social Studies grade needs to go up on the next report card. It's labeled "Just a friendly reminder".
8. Before meeting any parents, you are able to pick his haggard mother out of the crowd. She inquires hopefully about an extended school year.
9. You arrive at your classroom to find him relaxing in your chair, heels on the desk, "smoking" one of your flair pens, and demanding to know what kind of reward the class will get on Friday.
10. You find yourself rediscovering that earlier zest for teaching, ---and then realize he's been absent for two days.

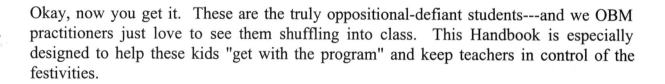

Okay, now you get it. These are the truly oppositional-defiant students---and we OBM practitioners just love to see them shuffling into class. This Handbook is especially designed to help these kids "get with the program" and keep teachers in control of the festivities.

Using Gender Pronouns

You have probably noticed that our student examples are presented in the male gender. Chances are, this doesn't bother you much at all; especially if you have just struggled through some required reading where the author kept switching back and forth at random between the gender pronouns. We're sensible down home folks and we do believe that both boys and girls should generally be used in educational examples. However, in the present Handbook, you will find that we have used the masculine gender when OBM techniques are described. Aside from continuity, we have an empirical basis for this presentation. Year after year, we have conducted a gender frequency count on our own student case loads. It may be no surprise to you, but we consistently discovered that over 85% of our most difficult oppositional kids wore blue booties when they were in the crib.

Underlying Principles of OBM

Number One: If It Ain't Broke....Don't Fix It!

OBM methods are unique, strategic, and sometimes labor intensive. If your regular classroom management procedures are sufficient, why change? Why use a fancy dynamite charge to lift your petunias when the old garden spade works just fine? I am reminded here of a staff consultation meeting where a notoriously difficult student was being discussed. One teacher had just reported problems with some pretty awful disruptive behaviors, and (because I was invited there as the "expert") I found myself beginning to mentally arrange some respectable inquiries which would guide the design of a behavioral intervention:

> *"Humm...Wonder if her time out consequence is too weak?...*
> *Maybe there's some uncontrolled social reinforcement for this*
> *behavior cycle?....Should we define some target behaviors and*
> *get started on baseline recording?.....uh, isn't it about time for lunch?...."*

Meanwhile, the next individual to report on this student was a no-nonsense veteran teacher who acknowledged that some of the same evil nasty disruptions had also occurred in her class. I recall one of our empathetic counselors say something like "Wow, that sounds pretty serious..." Without blinking, the veteran teacher responded, "Not really, I just told him to cut it out and get back to work." Her method was direct, non-technical, and effective. The moral of the story? Some situations don't require fancy strategies. If you already "have the power", just use it.

Once again, with feeling: *"If it ain't broke...don't fix it!"*

Number Two: If It Isn't Working....Stop Running It Into The Ground.

Has anyone figured out why some teachers live out decades of their professional career recycling their "Plan A" behavior management strategy that flat out doesn't work? Because oppositional-defiant students have the propensity to test the limits of our endurance, it is important that we be willing to let go of the old standbys. We may need to shut down our comfortable method of rational explanation and tactful redirection. From time to time we may even have to give up such classic tools as happy stickers, notes sent home, and raging threats of imminent destruction. Sure, these may work for other students, but they only bring a smile to the hard core oppositional student. To rephrase this important OBM principal, when your "standard procedure" doesn't work, stop whining and do something (anything) different.

Number Three: Work Smarter...Not Harder.

A teacher with a creative unconventional arsenal of management strategies is more suited to educate a strong-willed student. We can only feel sympathy for those well meaning teachers who wear an *Avis* button and endure more grief. And yes, there is a certain gleam of empowerment in the eye of that teacher who has discovered some effective OBM strategies. It's always a joy to behold the enthusiasm of workshop participants who have had some lights go on...and can't wait for Monday morning. We hope this handbook will put a special secure gleam in many weary eyes!

Number Four: The Next Best Thing To Compliance.....Is Confusion.

Think about this: It's hard to be mentally confused and rebellious at the same time. In managing resistant students, some use should be planned for strategically generated bewilderment, distraction, free floating anxiety, and internal disorientation. Moving targets are harder to hit and the teacher who is known to be occasionally unpredictable (i.e., *like a fox*) is less likely prey for the power crazed oppositional student. Many of the OBM methods presented in this handbook are meant to deliberately confuse those nefarious agendas and get our difficult students back to the learning process.

Number Five: Transform "Problems" Into Educational Projects.

As we journey through this unorthodox handbook, you will notice the absence of direct blame or assignment of fault for misbehaviors. We are quite aware that individuals do bear responsibility for their conduct. However, we are also aware that oppositional-defiant students have made an art form out of denial and rationalization. Because we would rather work smarter, we tend to avoid the barricaded front door and quietly slip through a side window.

Essentially, the OBM teacher develops temporary blindness to that disgusting resistance of the strong-willed student; and instead finds a way to make a helpful project out of it. The OBM teacher enters the classroom armed with a plan for transforming that disruptive target behavior into some "necessary" educational project. This will make much more sense later.

Number Six: OBM Doesn't Fit Every Teacher.

We have found that some teachers are temperamentally predisposed to instant success with OBM technology. Others are not. In most cases, our consultation meetings have been colored by honest laughter, the sharing of classic war stories about "oppositional students we have known"; and some very productive "possibility thinking". Our consultees generally leave with a packet of strategies under their arm, new resolve to lead their classroom, and a dangerous plan for tomorrow morning.

On the other hand we have found some rare allergic reactions to OBM stealth. I recall one extreme negative case with a hyper-assertive male teacher who sat to the rear of an elementary inservice workshop. With each new principle or strategy presented to the faculty, his hand would immediately go up.   He would then pronounce an argumentative "Yeah-but" question that highlighted some instance where a given method probably would not work.   As his unsolicited comments became less rational and intensified into red faced anger, I came to realize that the deeper strategic nature of some OBM methods may trigger unpredicted emotions in certain individuals.   We were never able to convert this guy.   I did eventually ask him to *help us out* by thinking of at least two practical problems for each new intervention.

It must be concluded that the strategic nature of OBM makes it incompatible with some personalities.   Interestingly, those who present extreme negative reactions (certainly much worse than yours) are probably the same type who would have profited from OBM interventions during their early school career. Hmmm, maybe that's it?

There is a lighter side to this compatibility thing. I recall some workshop evaluation forms with such insightful comments as:

"You guys ought to be locked up somewhere, for your own good."

"We <u>never</u> studied these things in graduate school."

"I'd require a five-day waiting period before allowing your OBM Trainees back into real classrooms."

"I'm just glad there were some good refreshments at this training."

Number Seven: If You Can't Extinguish It.....License It, Tax It, and Regulate It.

Some strains of nuisance behavior are quite resistant to total extinction. Not to worry. Instead of fighting them (which we never do in OBM practice); why not find a creative bureaucratic way to regulate them to death? In dealing with oppositional students, it may be just as important to "appear" to have control, as to actually have control. In these cases, the teacher appears to accommodate the evil behavior but adds the onerous burden of ridiculous regulatory paper work. Sounds like Big Brother already knows this one.

It's Time To Assess Your Own Compatibility With OBM Methods:

After lecturing and consulting with hundreds of teachers, I am increasingly convinced that our self-assessment exercise in Appendix I is still a very useful predictor of how any given teacher will "mesh" with strategic methods. Okay, so it's not psychometrically sophisticated. And yes, it may seem a bit goofy. But the self assessment exercise does speak volumes about an individual's OBM compatibility.

In addition to the contrived raw score, the informal attitudes and spontaneous reactions generated during this little exercise have pretty much reflected just how well a teacher will be able to understand, enjoy, and apply the OBM methods. We like to hand out this assessment sheet and then just stand back and listen to the chuckling or bewilderment. In just a few minutes we can identify those workshop participants who will excel.....and those who may need crisis intervention. If you have not yet done so, remove all books and papers from your desk, turn to Appendix I, and begin the test. You are on your honor. Good Luck!

Q: Can somebody here draw a picture of a very
        stubborn student who won't listen to the
        teacher, and never does what he is told to do?

        And here's our favorite 4th grade entry
        for your amusement.

Chapter Two

Could You *Pretend* To Be A Real Jerk?
The Classic OBM Paradigm

When Resistance Is Compliance:

This is the one that started it all. When set up correctly, the teacher takes almost immediate control of the problem behavior, no matter how the student chooses to respond. This intervention is built on a paradoxic request (i.e., "Could you

please help me out by pretending to be a difficult student?"). There is also an embedded double bind contingency. That is, the student becomes "compliant" when he performs the disgusting target behavior---or else he becomes "compliant" by refusing to perform the disgusting target behavior. Is this elegant or what? Yes, there are some required techniques to get it off the ground, but this one can show results the very first day. If you only buy into one OBM strategy this year, take this little puppy home.

In the early days of OBM development, we used some of the confidence game lingo that we vaguely remembered from the Redford & Newman movie: *The Sting*. Our workshop demonstration video was also the theatrical debut for one of our Special Education counselors who comprised the role of "Oppositional Eddy". This strong willed class wrecker took much pride in his defiance and even carved notches in his desk to keep track of how many of his teachers resigned during the year ---or had to be committed. At this point "enter, stage left" our mild mannered rookie teacher who should have been easy pickings for Eddy. Instead, Eddy became the focus of an OBM intervention that was narrated through such fanciful steps as: Choosing the Mark, The Set-Up, The Sting, and Cooling the Mark. Despite the fact that these steps were lifted from the movie, they were found to describe Eddy's "Sting" quite well. Our not-ready-for-prime-time video production showed helpless Eddy in his stages of metamorphosis. This student's proud career as the in-house problem child was largely neutralized and replaced with some semblance of classroom compliance. Below is a summary of the four steps in pulling off this powerful classroom intervention.

1. Choosing The Mark:

Not every student is a candidate for this particular intervention. We have found that the more deeply ingrained the defiance, and the more rigid the personality of the student;---the better this method actually works! In this case, one should not look for some easy student to practice on. Rather, the teacher should be encouraged to boldly target the most disruptive and defiant student in the class. After all, if this one student's behavior were to mellow out, wouldn't everything else in class go a lot smoother?

2. The Set-Up:

This is a critical part of the intervention. Ask your Oppositional Eddy to remain after class when there will be ample time to visit. In this brief private meeting, announce that you are working on developing one of your teaching skills (i.e., student motivation, classroom management, etc.)---and would really appreciate some help. Below are some sample scripts that have been tailored to specific problem behaviors. Once you get the idea, any one of the scripts can be adapted to fit a special target behavior. Take some time now and imagine yourself (with a straight face and innocent eyes) using one of the following scripts with your most oppositional student.

Sample Script #1
Excessive Talking In Class:

"I'm trying to practice my skill of handling students who talk too much in class. Is it possible that you might be willing to help me out during the next week or so? All I need is a student who would pretend to be a big time talker in third and fourth hour. If you could help me, all you would need to do is remember to talk and chatter away during these hours---so I can practice how to do effective warnings and reminders...and so I can make up tough consequences and stuff. Don't worry, if we run this thing right you won't really get into any big trouble. You'll be working "underground" and so if you get some kind of punishment, just act all upset as usual. It will be our secret and I'll see to it that you get released from it...like if you had to go to the office or something. In exchange for your help, I'll keep track of the days you help out and give you a pretty nice reward." (Explain a possible earned privilege or bonus points.)

Being Slow To Start Work Assignments:

"Thanks for staying after class a few moments. Here's what's happening. This semester I'm supposed to be working on developing some good classroom management skills. You know, us teachers are always supposed to be working on something. Anyway, I was wondering if I could count on you for a little extra help during English Class for the next couple weeks. I need to find a student who would pretend to work very slow so I can practice some motivational ideas. If you could help out, all you would need to do is be sure you are the very last student to start the written assignments...and then keep an eye on everyone else so you are always behind the rest of the class. Just keep creeping along like a snail. This would give me the opportunity to give you stern warnings and reminders---and maybe some kind of punishments. Oh, don't worry too much about the consequences. We'll make sure that you get out of them somehow when no one else is watching. It would be a personal favor to me, but I would also keep track of the days you help out and give you a pretty nice reward. (Discuss possibilities.) Well, is it a deal? Can we start on Monday?"

Sample Script #3
Resisting Class Rules And Teacher Instructions:

"I know how busy you are so I'll keep this short. This semester I'll be working on developing advanced classroom management skills. I need a really sharp student who would be willing to help me with my practice of enforcing the rules and controlling the class. This would have to be a secret deal. I thought you might be willing to help out. All you would have to do is pretend to resist certain class rules and also pretend to resist certain things I ask you to do (the teacher suggests possible rules or requests that might be resisted). Of course my job would be to give the usual warnings and try to get you to behave. You would make sure that none of my efforts work, even when I assign serious penalties. I'll check with you once in a while to see if my practice looks real enough. For each day that you help out I'll keep track and later slip you some nice reward. I'd like to work on my skills especially during the afternoon, but maybe some practice could be done in the morning if we could agree on a time."

Sample Script #4
Whining, Grumbling, And Complaining:

"I'm trying to practice my skills of handling student behavior problems in class. I really need to find one student who would pretend to grumble and carry on about the hard work or unfair rules...especially during first and second hour. If you could help me, all you would need to do is whine and gripe loud enough for others to hear you. Of course, it would have to look like real grumbling so that no one would know that it was just for training. Then I would pretend to get on your case and would be able to practice my get-tough skills. Don't worry, you wouldn't get into any real trouble. In fact, if you do a good job, I'll give you a pretty nice reward for your efforts. Is it a deal?"

Okay, you've picked up the general idea. Keep in mind that the "Set-Up" phase of this intervention is critical for creating the expectation of a mutual conspiracy. Frequently the oppositional student will not be too excited about helping the teacher "practice skills". If this got out, it might ruin his image. The student who feels silly performing *any* misbehaviors might be reminded that the deal is totally confidential. Of course it's always good for a few private chuckles to hear your disruptive student backing down and complaining that he would feel embarrassed to act like a total jerk in front of his peers. Nevertheless, it is important to stifle that smirk and keep up the sales pitch. The teacher might offer to give a secret signal (or use some secret word phrase) to alert a shy helper to do his thing.

Yes, It Gets Even Better!

I've never had a student totally refuse to "help me out" with some pretend misbehavior. Maybe this is due to my undiscovered charisma (not)...or most likely it's those incredible rewards (i.e., special privilege coupons) I offer as a pay off. Actually, my experience with refusals is mostly limited to marriage and family therapy situations where one member of the family system may adamantly reject the idea of pretending to have a symptom. No matter the reason for the refusal (e.g., embarrassment, denial that the symptom is a real issue, more jockeying for power, etc.), I usually plant the following "suggestion" and then casually go on to other matters:

> *"Maybe this assignment isn't quite right for the situation...or maybe it is.
> I'm not real sure. Let's just leave it this way. Go back into your world and
> live out some more days. If the assignment is right, your emotions and
> body will signal you to go through with it. If this assignment is actually
> important to do, you will know by the sudden realization that you have
> automatically jumped right into the behavior without even thinking about it.
> If you find yourself doing the "pretend" symptom behaviors, then just
> continue and do a good job...It means the assignment was right for you. If
> this never happens, we can work on other things..."*

Get the idea? When my client families are dealing with some deeply ingrained habit or behavior quirk (e.g., the suspicious and possessive spouse, the phobic client, the hypochondriac, the codependent, the "rageoholic", etc.) then it's only a matter of time before that nasty cycle kicks in and repeats itself---planning or no planning! We are safe to plant the suggestion, and then just wait.

18

With an OBM classroom intervention, I might apply the principle this way:

> *"Hey, I understand that this assignment is pretty difficult. It might even be embarrassing for some kids to pretend to do those problem behaviors. But I still really do need to practice my class management skills. Tell you what, let's just leave it this way for the coming week. You really don't have to do any of the behaviors we discussed. However, if for some reason, your mind sends down a message like 'Why not just pretend and help out!'...if you get that kind of thought in your head, and it just feels right to get into the behavior...Then just go ahead and do a good pretend behavior. I'll pick up on it right away, and begin practicing my behavior management skills. Later, I'll check back with you privately and see if you want to keep going. Sound Okay? So, if I see you do some good problem behaviors that look real, I'll know you decided to help out."*

3. The Sting:

After a successful Set-Up phase, the oppositional student will most likely offer some feeble efforts to "practice" the selected behaviors---or flat out "forget" to do the evil task. It is now very important for the OBM practitioner to keep a straight face while dutifully "prompting" the student to perform some daily practice cycles.

At this point the teacher should actively build more private collusion with the student. To do so will help to transform those disgusting little behaviors from cold harsh reality---to an "as if" level of fantasy and pretend...and even (choke on the word) "cooperation!" After all, isn't the disruptive tyrant now serving as an associate or secret operative for the teacher?

In order to foster a "this is our little secret" attitude toward the project, the OBM teacher might use candid winks or other secret signals to kindly remind the student to perform his stubborn or disruptive behaviors. For example, one teacher ran the daily sting by tapping the chalk on the board two times. It seemed like just a nervous habit or a way of emphasizing a point. Of course the oppositional student was well aware that it was the agreed-upon cue to let go with his usual disruptive comments.

Teachers who have used the *Pretend Jerk* intervention have stressed the need to "choose your signal wisely". In the heat of real world classroom dynamics, that secret signal is your only link to the problem kid. If he goes off the deep end, spaces out, wimps out, or goes ballistic with a major problem display, ...your signal is the only anchor for helping him get back with the "pretending" program. Remember, if this thing goes down wrong, *"The Secretary will disavow any knowledge of your activities......Good luck Jim..."*

Secret Signals:

Any kind of secret prompting method might be employed. Be sure you rehearse your signal until your student recognizes it easily amid the drone of regular classroom discourse. Consider some of these:

1. A commonly heard classroom teaching phrase might be a secret prompt.
    For example:
    "How much time do we have now?"
    "Are there any special questions?"

    ...Or how 'bout:
    "Class, what planet are we on now?"
    "Can anyone tell me why I'm employed here?"
    "What's the basic difference between a duck?"
    "About how long is a short road?"

2. An unobtrusive "clearing of the throat" type noise
3. A stifled yawn ...(no, these may be too common)
4. A pleasant smile or nod of the head directed toward the student
5. Placing a certain board eraser at some designated corner of the teacher's desk
6. Casually walking by and touching the target student's desk
7. How 'bout holding up a giant idiot card poster with bold print instructions? (maybe not)

Payment For Services Rendered:

So, what about reinforcers? The OBM teacher should consider using attractive daily payoff coupons to reward those semi-wonderful practice efforts. Did you ever dream that you might be lavishly rewarding a defiant student for performing such vexing behaviors? Well, after all, it is hard work resisting, disrupting, and pretending to be a difficult student. To get those creative juices flowing, the teacher might consult Chapter 11 which discusses the use of *Wacky Coupons and Behavior Permits*. We also offer some fairly non-traditional rewards in our *Student Reinforcement Inventory*, which is really a manic sampling of OBM payoffs presented in Appendix IV. Some kids would walk over hot coals for these silly things.

On the other hand, some more astute kids may still require jewelry, cruise packages, cash, or major appliances as reinforcers. Be reasonable, but consider how many weeks are left in the semester, and what some basic control is worth. One teacher weighed the cost of rewards against her HMO co-pay for psychotherapy sessions. At any rate, this is not the time to be cheap with solid reinforcement. It is recommended that some more-than-minimal reward be offered to energize this strategic intervention. It will send an important message to the oppositional student that the "pretend" behaviors are sincerely appreciated and important.

A Look At "Subtle Transformations":

We have found that, in order for this particular OBM intervention to be successful, it is important that the requested practice behaviors be slightly altered from their "raw form". The teacher must take some early control of the power crazed oppositional student by requiring slight shifts (almost "token changes") in the pretended annoying behaviors. You will want to check out Appendix III which is a summary of our *OBM Guide To Subtle Transformations*. If it is your intent to change the course of a mighty river (especially a rushing defiant one), you need to start early with some strategic erosion of the banks. Be sure to read this section! We put it in the Appendix section of the handbook so it would receive special attention and not get lost in the text.

Beginning with your Set-Up and continuing throughout the Sting phase, it is important that the teacher mix an ardent request for the defiant or disruptive behavior---with a good dose of Subtle Transformation. For example, it is not enough for Ms. Smiley to request that Oppositional Eddy pretend to whine about the hard work. Hey, this would be *identical* to what he already does every day. Rather, Ms. Smiley should select Eddy for her intervention, have her private Set-Up visit, and then add the Subtle Transformation of the symptom---almost as an afterthought: "Oh yes, and could you remember to always whine and complain a lot more during Reading Class?" (Or perhaps) "Oh, by the way, could you try to make your voice sound more sincerely concerned when you tattle on two kids from lunch recess?"

This early introduction of Subtle Transformations will accomplish two important goals. First, it quietly attaches some "busy work" or boundaries to those annoying behaviors that have always flowed reflexively from your oppositional student. Second, for our frazzled teacher, there is some early sense of control or empowerment added to the daily classroom situation. A request for even the smallest limits or change tends to offer the early "hope" that some eventual control is possible. It's satisfying to hear a teacher report *"Well, he's still a royal pain, but at least he's doing it on my terms!"* . That's the beginning of OBM control.

During the Sting phase, more and more subtle changes become "necessary" and the river of disruptive behavior is eventually channeled off in some benign direction. As more and more small changes are requested, the original disgusting behavior is distorted. and remolded into a completely different pattern. Okay, so it does sound a bit behavioral at this point...but it's still very outrageous.

4. Cooling The Mark:

The final phase of this particular OBM intervention is a graceful disengagement from the requested pretend behaviors. After all, we don't want to keep demanding resistance and defiance once the strong-willed student is ready to give them up. In the old time confidence rackets, they referred to "cooling the mark" as the phase where the slick operatives leave town on different trains and the target guy "never knew what hit him". In more humane terms, we might say that our OBM intervention has been successful if the stubborn defiant student is helped to let go of his disruptive behaviors and return to (or begin) some productive learning activities. He should continue to have a close working relationship with the teacher and not be burdened with any alienation or resentment. With all of our fancy strategic planning, *let's not forget that we really are trying to help the oppositional student*, even if he doesn't realize such help is needed.

Sometimes this final phase is accomplished almost automatically in a single day. Other times it is necessary to intentionally plan a quiet disengagement from the business of reinforcing all those silly pretend behaviors.

22

Some Slick Disengagement Ploys:

Below are a few suggestions for bowing out of the OBM game:

A. Begin to complain that your schedule is so busy that it's sometimes difficult to keep up with your skill practice---and hence the student's pretend behaviors might be wasted on those days.

B. Suggest that the pretend misbehaviors be performed "only for a couple minutes" at the beginning or end of class. These are obligatory acts that must be gotten out of the way each day.

C. Secretly conspire with the problem student to "skip" some practice days. After all, who will ever know?

D. Ask the student to double-up on his pretend behaviors, so that the two of you can take a break from practicing for a couple days.

E. Offer a "forced choice" dilemma to the strong-willed student: "Would you rather practice more often or less often this week?"

F. Apologize to the student for placing such a burden on his shoulders for so long. Ask if he feels that you have finally mastered the necessary classroom management skills. If so, then termination of his pretend behaviors would be a natural decision.

No doubt you have already thought out some of your own variations on "Cooling the Mark". Anything goes here as long as a good reason is supplied for terminating practice.

Rewards For A Good "Relapse"

We all know that your feisty student is going to "relapse" sooner or later. After all, he's had years to hone his intrusive and disruptive personality style. No problemo cousin Remo. In fact, future relapses of the target behavior should be predicted and pre-approved. Most of all, this new cooperative relationship with the teacher needs to be preserved and celebrated. As a way of Cooling the Mark, suggest an ultimate "final phase" of your skills practice. In this phase, the regular daily performance of misbehavior is suspended. Instead, the student agrees to "surprise" the teacher sometime in the near future with a classic misbehavior that *looks very real*. Check out our face-saving coupon for surprise relapses. Why not give a couple of these little cards to your "helper" and suggest he use them both within the next five days? This disengagement scenario allows the teacher to automatically place a benign interpretation on any future relapses ---and even thank the student for remembering to help out. (I see you grinning.) Now, imagine this relapse scenario:

> *The student reflexively blurts out some defiant comment while you are presenting the Science worksheets. You respond with a warning and a redirect, then turn to some other activity without further comment. The lunch bell rings and students begin to exit the classroom. As the student passes by you smile and hold out your ticket-taking hand. Your OBM target student slaps a relapse coupon in your palm. You then cautiously whisper: "That was a great surprise behavior...and it looked so real! Try me out again tomorrow, and let me know how I'm doing."*

Retirement Benefits

Just think, someday in the future while you're enjoying those fat social security checks, your most oppositional student might point to you rocking on your front porch: "See that burned out looking teacher over there?...When I was younger, I helped to train her in handling problem kids." You can almost feel that sense of civic pride well up as your defiant student recalls how he *pretended to be a jerk*...for a good cause. Can OBM get any better than this?

More Goodies On The Bottom Shelf

The following pages contain even more unnecessary resource materials which could further spoil you with this particular strategy. On the very last page of this chapter is a summary of the planning and implementary steps for the Pretend Jerk intervention. Sure, you hardly need these steps either, but we've been feeling rather codependent today.

WEEKLY CONTRACT FOR SERVICES

In order to help my teacher develop good classroom management skills, I agree to act out the exact behaviors listed in this contract. I understand it will be my teacher's job to practice some discipline and motivation methods on me while I am pretending to have these problem behaviors.

My Pretend Behaviors:

A. _____

B. _____

Daily Practice Session:

Time: _____

Place: _____

Reward Agreement:

My teacher will keep the Secret Assignment Credit Card in a safe place. Each time I act out a pretend behavior listed in this contract, my teacher will record 50 points on the card. I can earn up to 250 points each day for doing *pretend problem behaviors that look real* to my teacher. At the end of each week, I may purchase one (or more) of the items below with my earned Credit Card points.

Reward: _____ Cost: _____

Reward: _____ Cost: _____

Endorsement Signatures:

_____   _____
Student Assistant   Teacher

SECRET ASSIGNMENT
CREDIT CARD

⊕✈⊕✈⊕✈⊕✈⊕✈⊕✈⊕✈⊕✈⊕✈⊕✈⊕✈⊕

Student Assistant: _____

Pretend Behavior(s): _____

Credits Earned Today

Monday	
Tuesday	
Wednesday	
Thursday	
Friday	

Week #: ____ *Total Credits Earned This Week:* _____

Teacher's Endorsement : _____

Note: This card is confidential! It should be kept at the teacher's desk so all pretend behaviors can be credited. Only behaviors that <u>look real</u> can receive credit!

50 BONUS POINTS

Tough Act To Beat!

Fantastic performance!
Your pretend behaviors looked so real.
And your act was <u>very</u> helpful.

Here's one to add a little spice to daily "practice" efforts. Why not recognize an incredibly "real" looking performance? These coupons help to highlight the *pretend* nature of the assigned behaviors. They are given in addition to the regular earned points which the teacher records on the *Secret Assignment Credit Card*. Who knows, you might also convince the defiant student that he has a future in entertainment?

You might give your "graduating" student helper, a couple of these coupons so he can have some official means of alerting you to his surprise efforts. The next time he relapses into one of his reflexive misbehaviors, he can "save face" by handing you one of his coupons and claiming it was all part of the deal. *"Well.....e x c u s e.....me, that was only pretend..."* This, of course, allows the teacher to give some helpful critique and assign an offbeat subtle transformation for the next surprise! Good relapses are actually a sign of progress. They keep the cooperative conspiracy alive but low key. I love this stuff.

Could You _Pretend_ To Be A Real Jerk?

Summary of Steps

1. Choosing the Mark:

Be sure you are dealing with a hard core fire breathing oppositional-defiant student. No other kind will do here.

2. The Set-Up:

Arrange a brief private visit.

"Could you please help me practice my class management skills by pretending to act out a problem behavior?"
Discuss one or more fabulous rewards (See Appendix IV).
Be prepared for special handling of "refusal to be a jerk".
(Review details in the chapter)

3. The Sting:

This is the part where your helpful student performs the pretend misbehavior(s).

Complete your **Weekly Contract For Services**.
Do a brief role play of target behavior (optional, but wise).
Decide on a "secret signal" for prompting.
Record daily earned credits on the **Secret Assignment Card**.
Maintain a "mutual conspiracy" attitude with the student.
Gain some early control with a "Subtle Transformation" request.
"Oh, and by the way, could you remember to do the behavior this way...?"

4. Cooling the Mark:

You don't want to do this silly practice thing forever, do you?

Use a slick disengagement ploy to fade out the pretend misbehavior. (Review some of our options or ad lib your own)
Offer a reward for a future surprise "relapse" that looks real.
You know it's coming. It's better to be prepared & smiling.
Leave the expectation that more help with other pretend behaviors may be requested in the future.

Chapter Three

Rent-A-Thug
Placing the perpetrator on payroll

Employers Have More Clout Than Victims

Here's a good one for the "perpetually put upon" student who forever complains of mistreatment and unbearable teasing. We have found that it works equally well for the nice little kid who really has been targeted for classroom or playground harassment. Similar to other OBM interventions, this one makes a ridiculous project out of a disruptive symptom. Someone has observed that the Rent-A-Thug strategy takes a genuine subway mugging and turns it into a stilted choreography number from *West Side Story*. Here we will find our victim student hiring local muscle to "pretend" to hassle him---for some good reason. At any rate, this strategy shows how being an employer has it's privileges.

Setting The Stage:
In a brief private meeting with the victim student, debrief on the latest problem episode and then ask the following question:

> *"How would you like it if each time that bully called you a bad name, it would make you richer and richer?"*

This kind of out-of-the-blue question is intended to shock and disorient the victim student and make him open to unexpected suggestions. A more extended "possibility discussion" I have had with professional victims (or real victims) goes like this:

> *"How might you handle it if for each insult you got on the playground, or for each time someone teased you---a hired secretary of mine would stroll right up and hand you a sealed envelope with a $10 bill inside?....Each time a student would say anything unkind to you; oh oh, here comes my smiling secretary (who looks a lot like Vanna White) to hand you another envelope with some cash....I'm just wondering how many of those envelopes you might be holding by the end of one recess period? How 'bout by the end of the school day?....And how many insults and teasings might it take before you would have enough money collected to buy a new mountain*

bike? ....Would you be willing to ride that new 15 speed bike, even though you earned it by collecting insults at school?"....etc., etc.

It's Hard To Find Good Help These Days

During the private OBM interview with the student, I often lament the fact that the school really cannot give out envelopes with small amounts of cash inside, just for coming to school everyday and putting up with a lot of grief. (Well, actually they do, but the small sums are called faculty pay checks.) Anyway, it might be a good idea, but that kind of "soothing" and reparations for insult victims just isn't available.

From this off beat scenario I move on to suggest the "Rent-A-Thug" project where the victimized student earns token credits by secretly recording tally marks on an index card for each insult received during the entire school day. *It's actually better than this, because the victim student is also required to enlist one or two of the current bad guys to intentionally call him insulting names each day!* When enough tally marks are collected and turned in, the industrious victim student wins some special benefit, freedom, or classroom privilege.

Here's a suggested OBM script the victim might use to recruit the "help" of the top name-calling bad guys in class. Each one can be approached privately and individually (or, your professional victims may consult the whole bunch) with the following spiel:

(First our victim student checks to make sure that the bully and his associates aren't busy plundering or pillaging.)

"I'm working on a new program with the teacher (or counselor, principal, etc.) and I really could use your help! I'm studying about ways to handle feelings of anger or frustration that can happen when kids call me names or tease me here at school. I need to find a student who would be willing to call me names like _____ and _____ at least five times per day.

The way it works is that I'll record my "helper's" initials on a secret card and turn it in each day. The teacher then talks to me about what makes students say mean things to others, and how to handle any angry feelings. For each set of initials I mark on the card, I'll get 100 points! If I collect

enough insults for the week, then I'll win a pretty nice prize on
Friday...Can I count on you to call me some of those names at least five
times each day so I can start working toward the prize?"

Of course the victim student is coached to be very positive and to keep smiling while trying to enlist his Neanderthal thugs. This should not be a time to vent sarcasm on the bully student. In order to prepare the sales pitch, a few private role play scenarios are usually helpful. They need not take more than 45 seconds each. During this brief visit, the student and teacher might also reverse roles just to highlight both sides of an expected conversation. Remember, the tone must be wide-eyed innocence throughout the enlistment pitch. Everything must be optimistic and upbeat. Even if the bewildered bad guys refuse to cooperate (What? Withholding insults?) the victim should be prepped to keep smiling and leave them with a double-bind "open door" request:

"I know it sounds stupid to ask for insults. At least now you know why I
need them. If you change your mind during the next couple weeks, just go
ahead and call me some of those names we discussed (note: as usual!). *I'll*
know you've just decided to help me earn some points toward my prize."

Later, when that same old reflexive name calling mars an otherwise idyllic playground experience, the victim student can flash a knowing smile of gratitude, and quietly record the event on his card! At last, the sting of ridicule is replaced with the joy of cooperation.

Some Unnecessary Modifications:
(or, You OBM guys just don't know when to quit)

1. Give me your best shot!
The victim student might suggest (or insist upon) a specific list of the hottest derogatory names (which, of course, are already being thrown at him daily). It might be explained to the rented thug that only the most insulting names will do for this serious assignment. *"How else can a kid learn about the cruel world out there?"*

2. Tipping is permitted.
The "Victim" is earning big points for each insult, right? Why not suggest that he offer to share part of the reward with his rented thug. This might be a tactful thank you for helping out with this difficult assignment.

3. Practice makes perfect.

The "Victim" student could also invite the name-calling kid to one of the counseling/debriefing sessions so the teasing and verbal insults can be further role-played and practiced correctly. One part of this joint session might be a role-reversal exercise where the victim momentarily takes on the thug's role so as to demonstrate the proper intensity of the names he needs to be called. When the original roles are resumed, the thug is expected to be more sensitive and educated in just how to deliver those searing insults. The victim is then ready to critique the thug's performance. The moderating OBM teacher should also be sure to praise good approximations of the "critical skill" (get it?) in both students.

4. Recovery work.

Eventually the "Victim" student and a carefully selected team of name-callers might be enlisted to develop a guidance counseling demonstration of "how to handle teasing"---which is then presented to classes of younger students. Who knows, maybe the team could go on to offer a support group for students who are struggling to overcome the stigma and codependency of verbal insult cycles? Both victims and penitent perpetrators might be solicited for the group. By the way, what do you think has happened to the original name-calling problem that we started with?

5. Consciousness raising committee.

The newly formed recovery group might also be assigned the task of designing and making a counseling poster display which points out the evils of name-calling. Some reward or special privilege might be earned for the production of a good poster. Of course, much recognition should be given to the victim and recovering-perpetrator(s); and the poster might even be displayed somewhere in the school. Ambitious or workaholic teachers might want to go ahead and start writing that grant to fund a district-wide demonstration project; start selling those logo tee shirts, and raising money for the trip to Washington....No, no! Stop!, There is medication available for manic cycling OBM practitioners when things go this far.

At the heart of OBM methods is a playful reframing of the problem into an educational project. Notice that no one was punished or ridiculed in the Rent-A-Thug strategy. The victim student was never labeled as a powerless underdog who needed protection. Likewise, the name-calling nemesis of the playground was never acknowledged as anything but a voluntary helper. The OBM assignment made by the teacher or counselor allowed everyone to be approached with open innocent intentions. Eventually, the long standing cycle of verbal harassment was programmed into a benign charade.

OBM Legends

There are many compelling war stories that have been told about this particular OBM intervention. Over the years, small bands of teachers huddled around coffee pots in cold desolate lounges have found some encouragement in these tales. The Rent-a-Thug stories have now been retold countless times as an educator's oral tradition. While many of the original details have now been lost in the mists, the basic principles (e.g., reframing the problem and empowering the victim) are unchanging.

INSULT
COLLECTION CARD

Credits Awarded To:

....

Student Volunteers:_____

_____

These students will help in the program by doing teasing, insults, and name-calling during the regular school day.

Insult Credits Earned Today

Monday	
Tuesday	
Wednesday	
Thursday	
Friday	

Total Insult Credits This Week: _____

Teacher's Endorsement: _____

Save this card to earn fabulous prizes!

Here's our sample *Insult Collection Card* that's designed to transform our perpetual victim into a cheerful recipient of painless afronts. Make sure you've got some great back up reinforcers available to sweeten the deal. Take a gander at Appendix IV to help stimulate your creativity.

Chapter Four

Top Ten Strategic Responses
To Vile, Profane, or Gross Behaviors

Some Near-Genius Rejoinders

Remember the concept of "micro-management" that we mentioned in Chapter Two? What we are talking about here is the management of a specific face-to-face situation with the oppositional student that is carefully orchestrated so that the teacher holds some semblance of leadership and implicit control. As with the other OBM strategies, the Top-Ten Responses are not for daily use. They were never intended to hold a busy classroom on task. Rather, the gifted responses assembled in this chapter are intended for those difficult times when you really need something smooth and pithy to say. Instead of being caught flat footed and speechless, these classic comebacks are engineered to help the beleaguered teacher maintain control of the moment.

Teachers often report that they go through a private mental review of a difficult classroom situation (e.g., "How well did I handle little Bruno's tirade this morning?"). While this trivial drive-home exercise may resemble a post-trauma flashback for some teachers, it may also be a time of productive reflection on the day. We have all worked through one of these critical reviews and concluded "I sure wish I had said something really clear and elegant...I never seem to have the right words when I need them!" Sound familiar? Well, not to worry. This chapter is intended to get you rolling with some strategic responses that will keep you in control when other teachers might get worked up, red faced, and confrontational; or (worse yet) scared and sick, and retreating into their "wimp zone". Wouldn't it be pleasant to review today's problem episode with little Bruno and have a faint grin slip across your face? Wouldn't we all rather enjoy the replay and conclude, "Those were the perfect words for that situation!...I love it!....Just wish I had that one on video tape!" Welcome once again to the strategic world of OBM.

Think of it this way. Most of us take great effort to avoid dark alleys, late night parking lots, and certain streets in town. We don't like the feeling of vulnerability, and we prefer to keep our adrenaline stored up in some visceral gland where it belongs. Place us in the generic mugging situation and we'd feel helpless and distressed. Compare our intense anxiety with a soft spoken kung fu master who has walked into that same space. He may not want any trouble either, but he has at his command a vast repertoire of speeded precise movements that would neutralize the mugger and a half dozen of his accomplices. Despite an equal expenditure of adrenaline, our mild mannered kung fu fellow would probably have fewer post-trauma symptoms than we would.

Likewise, when the classroom teacher is suddenly confronted with vile, profane, or gross behaviors there is something a kin to an "assault" going on. These confrontive episodes represent a direct challenge to the leadership of the learning environment. We hope you will find one or more of our strategic verbal rejoinders to fit your style, and that you will feel much more comfortable dealing with your oppositional students. Read on grasshopper.

Classic Reframes

Reframing methods are found not only in our present chapter but throughout this manual. These are a way to take the raw behavioral event and reinterpret it in some other terms. It's like taking the same painting and enhancing the mood it creates by replacing the original low budget plastic frame with one that is gilded mahogany and much more complimentary. Fictional characters such as Mr. Magoo, and Inspector Clouseau are also adept at misinterpreting key events that are right in their face. If they did this intentionally, we might credit them with some pioneering work in Outrageous B-Mod.

Consider the myopic Mr. Magoo cartoon character. In one story segment we are shown a gnarly looking brut sneaking up behind Magoo, with a bat or club raised and ready to clobber him. Magoo turns around and chatters something like "Oh, you must be the gardener. Well, you're late sir!...And that rake you brought is much too short for all this work...yak, yak, yak..." The dumbfounded thug blinks helplessly at the audience as Magoo hustles him off to the garden while rattling on with several more absent-minded work instructions. We hope you find yourself smiling and considering that strategic "blindness" and creative "misinterpretations" can be useful and fun in the classroom. You'll find some interesting examples in the collection of strategies below.

Stealthy Distractions

Distraction methods take the spot light off of the "real" problem and place attention on some totally unrelated item. We've already mentioned Lt. Columbo's shrewd ability to "misinterpret" obvious clues in order to distract and draw out his sophisticated suspects. Beyond this, we all remember tense movie scenes where the bad guys seem to be in control and some clear thinking heroine feigns a fainting (say that fast several times). Anyway, that momentary distraction pulls all attention to a different level of reality (e.g., a minor medical crisis) and away from that ugly black revolver aimed at our protagonists. At this point Napoleon Solo, or Thomas Magnum, or James West ---is poised to seize the moment and turn the tables. Some of our strategic verbal responses act in the same way to defuse a tense moment and regain classroom control.

Planned Confusion

Beyond specific distraction episodes are broader global periods of deliberate confusion. At this point you may be drifting back to recall an early part of this manual where we announced that "The next best thing to compliance....is confusion". Some of our workshop teachers have raised their hand to confess that their classroom is *always* confused, with no controlling effect on the resident power monger. To this we must reply that all forms of confusion are not created equal. We are suggesting "planned" confusion that is purposefully orchestrated to achieve control in otherwise hopeless interactions. It's hard to be rebellious and disruptive when you are down right bewildered and disoriented. Even the most demanding and strong willed students will tend to mellow out when they are lost in a Twilight Zone rerun.

Hypnotists have used this planned confusion for years in breaking down mental resistance and creating their famous daydream states . The mind can only tolerate a limited number of incompatible thoughts at one time before it starts to shut down. Try to picture your most oppositional student looking up at you with a confused sick cow expression. This product of planned confusion may be your preferred low stress alternative to the usual classroom confrontations. We hope you will find some fertile inspiration among this chapter's sampling of strategic responses!

David Letterman, Move Over.

Okay, heeeere we go. Out of literally scores of witty entries gathered over the years, here is our top ten list of favorite strategic responses to vile, profane, or gross student behaviors. Since we don't have the stage band set up, and our drummer is in time out, let's just put some of our favorite ones up front.

1. *Hey man, That looks so real!*

(The teacher, obviously overcome with amazement and pedagogic pride) *"How do you make it look soooo real? You know, if a stranger were to walk in here just now and see you, he'd probably swear you were really upset about something!"* (The doting teacher walks on, talking to herself.) *"I'll never cease to be amazed with this class...There's more talent here than on most TV shows."* This is a great one for defusing such mood states as pouting, intimidating rage episodes, phoney alligator tears, and those hysterical reactions to a scraped knee. (Implicit message: You can't be serious.)

Now that you get the idea, let's slide on into some real zingers.

2. Come on now...Don't be so hard on yourself! You're doing just as well as anyone could expect!

(This is a "crazy maker" for defiant students who are geared up for mortal combat.) Right smack in the middle of a heated tirade aimed at destroying the teacher's leadership, the overly supportive instructor gushes some lines of syrupy encouragement. Here is a study in both distraction and benign reframing. Notice the teacher seems oblivious to the challenge and instead takes up the role of a sympathetic coach who is trying to help a favorite player save face or work through some personal defeat.

By the way, we could do another handbook for working with oppositional parents who storm into school meetings with rumblings of the Tasmanian Devil. This "supportive" response helps to tame down the Taz factor, and leaves these tactless disturbing folks standing there, mouth hanging open, blinking wide-eyed into the camera, and uncertain how to proceed. Meanwhile, notice that our mild mannered OBM teacher is totally supportive, smiling warmly, ...and no ill will has been projected. All other consultation options remain wide open, since no offense has been created. Hey, don't be so hard on yourself!

3. This is great! Well, at last you're able to get in touch with those deeper hidden feelings!

In this case, let's suppose that Oppositional Eddie has just lost his composure when his obviously superior health poster was not chosen for the special hallway bulletin board. In the midst of his whining and complaining, we see our proud teacher smiling in admiration as this complex student finds self-actualization right there in the classroom. After all, our emotionally constipated rebel has now been enlightened by gaining access to those deeper primal emotions. The teacher might enhance the approbation with something like: *"I'm really proud of you today Eddie! You know, sometimes a student has to risk looking like an absolute jerk, in order to bravely discover his true feelings. Your courage here today can be a model for all of us to follow."* (Here the OBM teacher begins to disengage and prepares to shift focus back to the learning activities. Like some of us who can't let well-enough alone, she just has to make a few more laudatory comments.) *"You're behavior here today is an example of how we should all learn to loosen up and let our genuine feelings flow like a mighty river! Next time Eddie, please don't hesitate to express your most primitive emotions....yak, yak, yak, etc."*

4. I don't care what everyone else may be thinking about you right now....

(Teacher glancing around at peers) *"I'm just glad that you're finally able to express those ugly feelings so well. This is great! Is there any thing more you need to say out loud?"* Here we catch a glimpse of a reality-bending technique where the teacher implies a special knowledge of the hidden thoughts of all others in the classroom. The unstated message is that "everyone" in class is watching with distain and condemnation. As students approach the adolescent era, they become even more vulnerable to that imaginary (and very critical) peer audience.

You may note that this implied knowledge helps to set up a double-bind message. On one hand, the OBM teacher is showing benign support and encouragement of the acting out behaviors ("Go ahead and cathart all over the place!"). On the other sneaky hand she is sending the message: "By the way, everyone here thinks you're a real geek when you act like this." So, do you like this one? Keep in mind that it's also a no-lose request. If the oppositional student insists on more time to blow smoke and noise, the teacher wins (i.e., he's following her invitation and instructions). Of course, if our defiant scholar refuses to continue, the teacher could also live with the silence. Think this one through carefully, and work on your presentation. Why not practice on a grumbling faculty member who hasn't read this handbook yet?

5. *It's truly amazing how well you control yourself during these tense times!*

Here's one of our favorites for those special moments when a student (or attitudinally challenged colleague) is in the middle of a temper display. Following the model of our myopic Mr. Magoo, the teacher becomes blind to the disruptive tantrum, and instead heaps praise on the red-faced angry student for showing such *relative* strength, control, and restraint. The follow-up chatter might go something like: *"You know, a lot of other kids would really lose it if they had to put up with the same stuff you get here everyday! How do you manage to stay so cool....I mean do you have some secret thing you say to yourself? or something special you do?"* As you can see, this one's a clever reframe which offers a benign interpretation of the facts. It gives the teacher some enhanced control of the situation and an opportunity to keep teaching.

I unashamedly use this approach with irate parents who are looking for blood. In such cases, I try to separate myself from the school establishment (always a good idea when you sense heat) and commiserate with the frustrated parents. Some of the parent talk might go like this: *"You guys must be real saints! Even with all this stuff (name the problem) you just keep on cooperating with this school. Why do you keep on helping and hoping? A lot of parents would have given up long ago. What's so different about you folks?..."* Usually at this point the angry parents seem to recover a bit and take their finger off the launch button. They most often accept my evaluation of their long term forbearance and then openly discuss how much they have suffered at the hands of the school district. Our informal conversations usually take place before the "real" meeting. We then collude on solutions that the parents might present when those real educators finally show up for the meeting.

6. Hey, why don't you go a little easier on your Mom!

This is a distraction method that also includes confusion and an off-the-wall interpretation. The assumption is that the OBM teacher knows the "real" reason for the student's oppositional posturing. She then points the spot light away from the problem behavior to the struggling mom, dad, custodial grandparent, or some other major player. The standard dialog continues with pedantic finger wagging and sympathy-seeking for the parent: *"Don't be so hard on your mother! I'm sure she's doing the very best she can. C'mon, cut her some slack. It's not easy being a parent these days...yak, yak, yak... In fact, every time I see you getting into this kind of trouble* (i.e., like for the millionth time this week) *I know there's still a lot of 'thank you's' and 'I'm sorry's' that you need to send home to your dear old mom...."*

Oddly enough, mothers don't seem to mind the use of this ploy. Also, from time to time it might be a good idea to assign a letter writing consequence so that the student can begin to balance that ledger of long over due sentiments to his mom. Notice how the focus has changed from the defiant episodes to the trumped up solution of showing more gratitude to a parent? I use this one when I'm real sure there isn't any gross abuse or neglect at home. Most often this isn't the issue with our classic oppositional defiant students. On the other hand, I could understand why some good-but-frustrated moms might be tempted to lean a bit in that direction.

7. Hey everyone, stop laughing! Maybe this kid can't help it! I've seen cases like this before.

Notice the implications here. First, the OBM teacher's comments suggest that "everyone" of the peers is laughing at our strong-willed student---either openly or (worse yet) privately. Second, the diagnosis of some unknown clinical syndrome and lost volitional control is offered as an explanation for the crying or cussing or book slamming episode. After feigning to hush-up the class, the teacher might turn supportively to the troubled student and add *"Do you want me to try and explain your situation to these other kids while you calm down?...Or is it none of their business?"* This forced-choice question suggests the classroom tyrant actually wants to calm down now. It is also skewed in the direction of admitting to having some strange unspeakable problem ---while insisting it is no one else's business. Oh the joys of language crafting!

Of course there's still the risk that a gifted oppositional student might call your bluff and have you "explain" his unique clinical syndrome. In this case, it might be best to act real embarrassed (for the student) cover your mouth suddenly and turn away. Hesitantly suggest you really don't know a lot about it but there are specialists who study that syndrome. They might be willing to visit privately with the student. On the other hand, if you're feeling a bit feisty, you might rattle off a few of the key symptoms: swollen ear lobes that draw fluid off the brain, irresistible impulses to flap the gums, a denial of having any problems, and bad breath. Yes there's several more tell tale symptoms but they would be just too embarrassing to announce in public. Besides, the clinical research remains inconclusive. At this point, if you feel a need for more "psycho-babble" support, just rush on to Chapter Six.

8. Are you Okay? You don't look too good at all.

This strategic response is similar to #7 (above) except the concern is for medical wellness rather than some unknown mental health problem. Supportive, gushy, codependent teachers should be especially adept at this one. Here again the teacher ignores the negative behavior and diverts attention to something else---the student's apparent illness (which might be causing the problem behavior).

The concerned teacher might extend the monologue with: *"Oh my, you are getting sick...Do these spells happen often? Would you like to see the nurse, or maybe lie down for awhile? (Looking puzzled and bewildered) Is there anyone I should call when these episodes happen?"* Hopefully, these caring inquiries are enough to break up the gross behavior episode and also put the teacher back in control of the classroom.

By the way, this is also a great distraction strategy for haggered principals who must deal---one more time---with that malcontent teacher at the end of the hall. It works even better if you have one or more staff members standing nearby---who immediately agree with the principal and offer to dial 911.

9. Aren't you afraid you might hurt my feelings when you say those kind of things?

This one could be worth some confusion and shock effect---especially with oppositional kids who maintain some vestiges of social morality. Here the OBM teacher holds forth the highest expectations for the sterling character of our defiant student. She presents surprise and disbelief that this student would ever remotely consider demeaning the character of another human being.

The implication is that there must be some obvious mistake: *"This just isn't like you....I'm shocked and saddened that something has pushed you so far...I know it would have to be very serious...because some of those comments might be possibly construed as hurtful by the people who heard them."* At this point, the teacher might offer to place the student's name on her prayer list, or provide some inspirational reading material.

Essentially, this strategy is based on the production of "cognitive dissonance" in the student (i.e., creating internal mental conflict by pointing out the extreme difference between his exemplary character---and this confusing sample of actual behavior).

10. Okay, which one of you guys is making my friend Bill here say these crude things?

Here's another wonderful distraction: Blame classroom peers for the problem behavior episode! *"Who is it that's making a good student like Bill feel so lousy that he has to say these rude and crude things?"* The teacher pensively scans the classroom, considering who the perpetrator of Bill's pain might be.

Two blame options might be used: First, the OBM teacher could fault one or two students who are totally uninvolved. She might wonder out loud whether these shadowy characters could be involved in some kind of mind-control conspiracy. *"Hmmm....Yes, that might be it. They could be trying to make a nice guy like Bill lose his cool and vent obscenities in class. I wonder how they do it?"*

A second option is to vehemently blame one of Bill's own gang! This opens up the *divide-and-conquer* ploy which we will discuss later in the handbook. The teacher might split Bill away from his oppositional colleagues with such banter as: *"Look, we all know that Bill is not the problem student here. You guys are always trying to set him up for trouble. I'm surprised he even hangs out with you anymore. For your information* (directed at the tough guy circle) *most of the teachers in this school really like Bill and all the improvement he's shown this year. We know he gets blamed for stuff you other guys are doing...and we're watching very close these days. Bill, you don't have to rat on your friends. I know it's not really you who wants to say these gross things in class. I ought to bust these other two guys right now, but I won't....just out of respect for all you've been putting up with this year..."* Kinda brings a tear to the eye, doesn't it?

48

Another Parting Shot

Okay, some of these rejoinders may be far fetched (understatement). We just hope you found one or two that will help you save your leadership credibility when little Rocky cuts loose next time. Keep in mind one of the key OBM principles discussed earlier: *The next best thing to compliance...is confusion.*

Strategic Responses
To Vile, Profane, or Gross Behaviors

Summary of Witty Techniques

1. Reframes:
Take the raw behavioral event and reinterpret the meaning---so as to disarm the aggressor. If the vile behavior was intended to embarrass, intimidate, or disrupt the teacher, find some way to see it as a sincere compliment, a sign of educational progress, or some latent talent.

2. Distraction:
Offer a quick rejoinder that changes the focus from the "real" problem to some totally unrelated and harmless topic. Find ways to ignore the malevolent intent of a defiant or gross behavior and focus instead on your disgust for untied sneakers, bad grammar, or emerging flu symptoms.

3. Planned Confusion:
Upon detecting the first signs of defiance---use preemptive distractions to generate mental chaos and bewilderment in the problem student. Use deliberate "crazy-maker" statements, announcements, and questions to stifle rebellious mental energy. "I know what you were thinking yesterday, and it's all opaque..."

Chapter Five

Gripes & Excuses Some Kids Use

More Fun With Oppositional Students

Have you ever been totally fed up with the endless excuses generated by your strong-willed students? Some kids can be caught red handed before a host of witnesses, and video taped from three angles performing their misdeed...and *still* come up with a list of self-vindicating excuses. Maybe they learn this stuff from network news coverage? Anyway, oppositional-defiant students do have extreme difficulty acknowledging their weaknesses and offering apologies. On the other hand, the ingenious defenses of their actions and smoke-screen complaints about injustice could rival any

media driven court room rhetoric! Some kids have to work at it, others are "naturals" with excuses. This chapter is focused on those few innately gifted excuse-makers found in most classrooms.

Since you are still with us into Chapter Five, you are already savvy enough to expect a different reaction to the chronic excuse makers. We will not be recommending that you jump into the ring with your champion whiner and try to spar with something so crude as logic and reasoning! Rather, we are going to discuss a way to commiserate and collaborate with your strong-willed student in lamenting his plight. Just think of all the rotten boring things he has to do, isn't allowed to do, or may be frustrated with! It's enough to make a kid qualify for the "attitudinally challenged" class.

Yes, there are so many bad things happening that it's easy to forget some of them. It's our suggestion that you help your oppositional student keep his stubborn resistance well organized and properly focused. To accomplish this, we recommend that you join with your creative student and assign some daily list making "opportunities".

List Making,...ad nauseam

Phony premise #1: Sometimes an oppositional student might become nervous and overwrought due to an unconscious fear of forgetting or overlooking some of the bad things in his world. To some obsessive-compulsive students, keeping a personal list of frustrations is almost like "controlling" those same frustrations. However, great volumes of psychic distress might be generated if the afflicted student were to lose track of his many gripes and they were allowed to become free floating within his character structure. Huh?

Phony premise #2: One teacher explained to Mid-school Mike that his classroom adjustment problems stemmed from "poor cognitive organization" of the many sources of threat to his self-esteem. Somehow, poor recall of his many life stressors was linked to having bad luck and conduct problems.

Phony premise #3: Some unfortunate students are hypersensitive to the multiple social and emotional irritants in the classroom environment. These students tend to internalize almost every source of frustration. Eventually, the pressures of everyday life build up just like a shaken bottle of Dr. Pepper---and spray all over the counter top and their new T-shirt. The solution to this plight is to allow for frequent controlled catharis (e.g., list making work). Sure, that sounds credible enough. As a benign support for keeping his mental world organized; or as a reinforcement of faulty memory skills; or even as a catharis opportunity, our impossible student might be asked to spend five minutes *at the beginning* of each day brainstorming lists of those frustrating life events.

Depending on his sad and disturbing life experiences, he might be required to generate a compelling inventory of unfair situations, angry feelings, or even his own diabolical threats and excuses. Previous days' lists might be reviewed in order to keep those negative items fresh in mind (of course, earlier items could not be repeated on future days' lists). This helpful assignment has been a real growth experience for many contrary natured students. Hey, it must be helpful since it puts the teacher in a leadership role.

Our OBM teachers also seem to get a kick out of the assignment. When a week of list making is completed, a copy of the resulting master inventory can be kept for both teacher and student reference. As our subject student eventually drifts back to his old ways, the teacher can offer to place frequency tally marks by his favorite items. This will allow her to keep track of which bellyaches or excuses seem to come up most often.

These helpful lists also allow OBM teachers to give meaningful feedback to their whining students. We have heard such comments as *"Looks like old # 12 is most popular again today!"* or even *"What happened to #5 and #17, we haven't heard them for days in first hour class?"* Remember, next to being compliant, our oppositional students hate to be considered predictable or analyzable. To be "understood" is seen as a sign of weakness. To be "figured out" suggests a chink in the armor that must be resisted at all cost. I have actually seen hard core stubborn kids give up a major (i.e., favorite) disruptive behavior simply because it was pointed out that they were "...like, totally predictable".

The Set Up

Instructions for this assignment can employ any rationale you prefer. You can cite a need for handwriting practice, long term memory support, emotional catharsis, or even some fancy computer exercise. Basically, the student is given some good reason why the list making is necessary. He is then required to sit at a certain desk each day until he has brainstormed three to five new items for his list. Often the assignment goes on for a full week or until a total number of items are generated (say, two or three thousand?).

Overly conscientious OBM teachers have been known to keep a few of these classic titles (i.e., prepared blanks) in a folder and ready for use when needed. By the way, is it really an underhanded threat to suggest that the student's folder of whining topics and pet excuses might be passed on to next year's teacher? Of course, OBM teachers are not above supportive black mail, if it's used strategically to support the learning process.

To get things rolling, the assigned topic of concern is printed at the top of a page and numbered spaces are indicated for the daily quota of gripes and excuses. Students may need to be reminded that they can't repeat any item---despite how good and juicy a particular one may seem. To stimulate your imagination, we've included a list of common topics. At the end of the chapter you will also find that a few of these have been transferred to worksheets for a week-long brainstorming assignment. These particular forms have already seen action with some of those perpetual whiners and "excuse making" buffs among us.

Sample List-Making Topics:

1. More examples of why life isn't fair in this class.
2. Immature and annoying things that some other kids do.
3. Reasons why I always get blamed for things.
4. Some lifelong benefits of quitting this stupid school.
5. Some evil, terrible things I hope will happen to this school.
6. How I would change the unfair rules in this class.
7. Honest reasons why homework might not get done.
8. Violations of student rights I have seen around here.
9. Some benefits of arguing for your rights.
8. Student behaviors I have endured: Geeks, nerds, & punks.
9. Methods I've used to stay awake in this boring class.
10. Some ways this class reminds me of a prison.

A Few More Reasons
WHY I ALWAYS GET BLAMED FOR THINGS!

Your assignment is to create a list of "Reasons" for the problem above. Use your own miserable life experience in this class to think of as many answers as possible.

Student: _____ Class: _____

Monday:
1. _____
2. _____
3. _____

Tuesday:
4. _____
5. _____
6. _____

Wednesday:
7. _____
8. _____
9. _____

Thursday:
10. _____
11. _____
12. _____

Friday:
13. _____
14. _____
15. _____

Some Lifelong Benefits of
Quitting this Stupid School!

Your assignment is to create a good list of "Benefits" for the problem stated above. Use your knowledge of adolescent and older drop-outs to help you think of real benefits.

Student: _____ Class: _____

Monday:

1. _____
2. _____
3. _____

Tuesday:

4. _____
5. _____
6. _____

Wednesday:

7. _____
8. _____
9. _____

Thursday:

10. _____
11. _____
12. _____

Friday:

13. _____
14. _____
15. _____

Some Honest Reasons
WHY HOMEWORK MIGHT NOT GET DONE

Your assignment is to create a list of "Reasons" for the problem stated above. Use your own personal observations in this difficult class to help you think of some good answers.

Student: _____ Class: _____

Monday:
1. _____
2. _____
3. _____

Tuesday:
4. _____
5. _____
6. _____

Wednesday:
7. _____
8. _____
9. _____

Thursday:
10. _____
11. _____
12. _____

Friday:
13. _____
14. _____
15. _____

How I Would Change The

UNFAIR RULES IN THIS CLASS

Your assignment is to create a list of "Changes" for this sorry classroom. Use your own bad experiences here to help you think of as many ideas as possible.

Student: _____ Class: _____

Monday:
1. _____
2. _____
3. _____

Tuesday:
4. _____
5. _____
6. _____

Wednesday:
7. _____
8. _____
9. _____

Thursday:
10. _____
11. _____
12. _____

Friday:
13. _____
14. _____
15. _____

Rude Behaviors I Have Endured From:

Geeks, Nerds, & Punks

Your assignment is to create a list of the most "crude and disgusting" behaviors you have experienced in the cultural wasteland of our school. Try to remember your very worst social encounters and most humiliating memories to record below.

Student: _____ Class: _____

Monday:
1. _____
2. _____
3. _____

Tuesday:
4. _____
5. _____
6. _____

Wednesday:
7. _____
8. _____
9. _____

Thursday:
10. _____
11. _____
12. _____

Friday:
13. _____
14. _____
15. _____

More Examples of
Why Life Isn't Fair In This Class!

Your assignment is to create a list of "good examples" for the disgusting situation stated above. Use your own bad experiences in this class to help you think of answers.

Student: _____ Class: _____

Monday:
1. _____
2. _____
3. _____

Tuesday:
4. _____
5. _____
6. _____

Wednesday:
7. _____
8. _____
9. _____

Thursday:
10. _____
11. _____
12. _____

Friday:
13. _____
14. _____
15. _____

Chapter Six

Playing Sigmund Freud In The Classroom

Your Crash Course in Psychoanalysis

Just as you can learn all you really need to know about life in kindergarten, so too your life quota of psychoanalytic skills can come from a few classic movies. Honest. If you have seen *Psycho*, the *Three Faces of Eve*, and maybe *Dr. Jekyll and Mr. Hyde*; you have all the fundamental concepts for psychoanalytic work. Well, Okay, there must be a few deeper principles not covered in these movies, but you'll get enough from them (and perhaps an afternoon of network talk shows) to sound credible in your OBM work.

Basically, psychoanalytic thinking has done a thorough job of convincing our culture that nothing is (really) as it appears to be. All human behavior is the product of swirling shadowy unseen psychological forces battling each other and struggling for expression. No one ever performs an asocial act because they simply intended to do something bad. There is no "bad" anything for which one might be culpable. We are all victims of unresolved "conflicts". Freud and his followers could see primitive sexual drives, parental enmeshment, fixated development, and a host of shadowy complexes and neuroses in even the simplest of behaviors.

....And now you too can start seeing these deeper forces in everyday contacts with your most difficult students! Keep in mind that these strong willed students are also very brittle. Power is their game and they do not want to reveal anything "personal" that could possibly be exploited. Oppositional kids loath the idea of "being understood" or being "read like a book". When OBM teachers arrive on the scene with their supposed deeper understanding of the student's developmental plight, it can be a real threat to the power agenda.

Hanging Out Your Shingle

If you hale from a much earlier, kinder and gentler decade, you may recall the Ricky Nelson song which declared that "fools rush in where angels fear to go". (I only know this one from the oldies station. Honest.) Anyway, this lyric may offer some food for thought before hanging out your OBM shingle with jolly old Sigmund. We are suggesting that teachers can gain some control of the oppositional student by making off-the-wall interpretations of his classroom behavior. We are not suggesting that actual---perhaps very real and painful---material be mirrored to the student as an explanation of his problem behaviors. As the song states, only a fool rushes in (and breaks open Pandora's Box).

So, how does the OBM teacher draw the line? My first response would be that the teachers who should use this particular strategy are *those who already know* where to draw the line. For you, there is an intuitive sense of fair play, of close enough but not cruel, of witty but not damaging. More on the ethics of OBM in a later chapter. From a more pragmatic perspective, you don't have to dig up real dirt on your impossible student. We have found that crazy, confusing, and unlikely interpretations of behavior seem to work just fine.

In the pioneer days of OBM I had some favorite scripts of canned interpretations ---primarily for the vulnerable but impossible middle school tough guys. Apparently some body-pierced burglars or mid school gangsters have now broken into my office and (oddly enough) stole just those classic scripts. Not to worry. This part of the chapter could blossom out of fond memories alone.

Using "Assumed Knowledge"

Oppositional students come in different packages. Some are a royal pain but have other redeeming qualities that endear them to you. Dave fit that description. He was a tall blonde kid with a high verbal IQ, some kind of a mild learning disability, and a deeply felt mandate to argue any issue from pro sports to student rights. I still liked him. Dave also had a dozen entertaining explanations for any of his classroom disruptions. In my weekly counseling work and classroom visits, it became apparent that Dave was slightly paranoid and highly suggestible. This helped a lot when I started digging in my ideas bag to select an OBM strategy.

One week I met with Dave and was prepared to ask the following list of interview questions: (Picture this poor oppositional student trying to figure out what was cooking.)

> *What's your actual exact age today?* (I then computed it on paper while mumbling, *"Uh huh, just as I thought".)*

> *Have you had any unusual dreams lately---that you can't remember too well?*

You had a growth spurt over the Summer. Are you tall as your dad yet?

Do you sometimes get the impression that things aren't real? Like maybe the world isn't really real. Hmmm.

Have you noticed that your stomach sometimes growls or gurgles when you sit toward the front of the class in Social Studies? (I knew his seat placement in the class just before lunch.)

Have you noticed any times recently in the hallway when (for no apparent reason) other kids have looked at you with just a very slight---almost unnoticeable---expression on their face?

Over the past two weeks have you lost some small items at school that nobody remembers seeing?

Is it possible to lose something and not remember you did? (Just as he denied the possibility, I handed him his own chewed down Bic pen which I had lifted a few minutes before the interview---all without comment.)

Okay, you get the idea. Actually, I had a much longer list of unusual inquiries that helped me develop a supposed psychological "profile" of Dave's situation. While maintaining some detached clinical objectivity, I sketched out a two axis graph and zig-zagged a line across a dozen unnamed scales. I then commented to my oppositional adolescent that such a profile might be useful in predicting "irresistible future changes". As you might guess, this stubborn, slightly paranoid student was immediately interested in what the forthcoming predictions might be. At the same time he tried to muster some skepticism and arguments that such predictions just wouldn't work for him.

Polymorphous Adolescent Development Test

Let's suppose you're just too busy to dream up a bunch of vague interview questions like the ones I used with my stubborn middle school client. There are other ways to generate some "assumed knowledge" of that willful adolescent's fragile psyche. You might use a venerated psychoanalytic test such as the *Draw a Moody Cloud;* or the family systems assessment instrument: *Draw-Your-Family-Coming-Home-From-Wal-Mart.* Maybe you would prefer my old projective favorite: *Draw-a-Microwave-Oven.* If you're in a pinch, just take a clean Scott Towel and wipe down a table in the teachers' lounge (preferably after a rich pasta lunch). Carefully spread out the used paper towel before the bewildered student and ask him to free-associate to all the unusual colors, designs, and smells. Take careful notes, do a few clarifications, and suddenly you have a wealth of knowledge about his current developmental crisis.

If you prefer a paper and pencil written exercise, we submit the *Polymorphous Adolescent Development Test* for your thoughtful consideration. Our committe generated instrument is presented here in it's entirety for your amusement and possible use. This test has absolutely no psychological meaning. It's merely a collection of vague items which may include some familiar content for those caught in the thralls of adolescence.

Test Administration Hints

If you choose to administer this test, always do so with cool clinical objectivity. Assure the student that this instrument will generate information helpful in planning his school life. Stress that the results will be confidential and that he will be fully debriefed once the elaborate scoring and interpretation has been completed. Although this isn't a "real" test of anything, our OBM staff has been diligent in seeking counsel on it's proper use. We have been assured by the A. E. Newman law firm that our "Polymorphous" measure of development ranks with many other classics carried in those tabloids "for inquiring minds".

POLYMORPHOUS ADOLESCENT DEVELOPMENT TEST

Adapted from the work of international scholars in polymorphous development
Barry T. Christian, Ph.D. (1997)

Name: _____ Age at time of testing: _____

Instructions: This exercise is unlike other school tests you may have taken. The items below have no right or wrong answers. Rather, these questions will help to determine where you are in the many areas of normal adolescent development. This test is "polymorphous" because it measures many parts or forms of character development. Try to give the first or second response that comes to your mind. Total honesty is not important with this sophisticated test.

1. I have never found myself wondering what it would be like to be someone different.
   Answer: T or F
2. My earliest memories seem to be stored as:
   Answer: Color Photos   Black & White Photos   Video Without Sound   Any Others
3. When I wear green or blue clothing it makes me feel most comfortable.
   Answer: T or F
4. I can recall a time when I squeezed as many as six quarters together between my thumb and forefinger.
   Answer: T or F
5. I have written poetry without understanding it's true meaning.
   Answer: T or F
6. I am quite sure that I have had some unusual dreams in the past year.
   Answer: T or F
7. Old familiar smells, odors, and aromas can easily cause me to daydream.
   Answer: T or F
8. During a regular school day I have noticed the same *written number* reappearing at different times or places.
   Answer: T or F
9. When I am resting, my eyes often come to focus on square or rectangular objects.
   Answer: T or F
10. When I am nervous, my eyes seek out earth-tone or wooden objects to stare at.
    Answer: T or F
11. When walking in the school hallways, I have noticed some students watching me with no real expression on their face.
    Answer: T or F

12. Place a circle around the symbol which makes you feel most safe.
13. Place a triangle around the symbol which seems most chilled or cold.
14. Underline the symbol which most reflects your hidden personality.
15. Cross off the symbol which is most upsetting or disturbing to you.

Cryptic Interpretations

These are the rare moments a teacher should relish. Despite where you dig up the psychological "goods", why hurry to give Dave (or your own strong-willed counterpart) a lot more information? Why jump into predictions and helpful "therapeutic" assignments? Sometimes we need to just let our bird stew a while longer before serving.

Our homespun clinical "profile" must be vague enough to support just about any interpretation. The very best ones will be as nebulous as a syndicated horoscope or a psychic hotline script ....no specifics, just things that *sound* specific. Once you have plotted the data and eye-balled the student's profile, it's time to stare pensively into space, mumble some esoteric words to yourself, and then offer the student some deep OBM insight.

Below are a few sample interpretations you might consider. Notice that none of them involves mean spirited labeling or direct confrontation about the real classroom problems. You won't see any objective diagnoses (e.g., "You talk back too much. You never start working on time. (or) You're basically a pain to deal with each day"). Remember OBM Principle #3: *Work smarter, not harder.* These sample interpretations show how you can get passed that tough oppositional armor and closer to that insecure central core. To do this we create a problem or "issue" that is totally off in left field. Now that you have the benefit of "deeper insights" from your interview or test scores, these oddball clinical ramblings can be presented with the flourish and authority of a *Verbal Advantage* graduate.

In the items below, watch for (and savor) the empathetic mood tone of the OBM interpretations. Here we see the teacher as a warm, knowledgeable sage who is simply offering a bit of insight and guidance. Cool, right?

Try some of these debriefings on for size:

> *"You seem to be entering a stage of punctuated psychological equilibrium. In fact this profile suggests maybe two or three levels of personality metamorphism. Look here at the angle on these triad factors. That's really amazing."*

"You're definitely well into Stage III of neuro-social confabulation! That's really a critical phase that will demand a lot of your energy. Especially at this grade level. Of course there are always some special cautions and concerns at this stage. Have you ever read any of the neo-analytic writers?"

"Looks like you've successfully negotiated the two fundamental adolescent crises of attitudinal cathexis and early identity lamination. These are both

latent developmental milestones that are essential to future archetypal disposition. Wow, and you're only 14 years old!"

"This profile shows the classic lines of both the retentive and expulsive prototaxic modes. See the difference here between these highs and lows? No doubt a clean sublimation of ascetic drives. I'm not easily impressed, but this is exemplary."

Psycho-Babble Verbiage Generator

So this looks intriguing or maybe just entertaining, but you couldn't possibly dream up all that psychoanalytic verbiage. Besides, the defiant kid you're presently thinking about would need more than the proverbial "snow job", he'd require some kind of a blizzard to get him confused. Again, not to worry. Hey, we'll take care of you. You just need some convincing terminology to craft your "interpretation" of student behavior. Check out our verbiage generator. Along with our Polymorphous test, it's another great support tool for OBM practitioners, (and wannabees).

𝕻𝖘𝖞𝖈𝖍𝖔-𝕭𝖆𝖇𝖇𝖑𝖊 𝖁𝖊𝖗𝖇𝖎𝖆𝖌𝖊 𝕲𝖊𝖓𝖊𝖗𝖆𝖙𝖔𝖗

Feeling slow on the draw with those phony psychiatric terms? Join the club. What you need is a whole new menu of psychoanalytic excuses for human behavior! Just choose three random numbers from 1 to 9. Enter each column and find the corresponding word. Simply link your words together, state them with confidence and authority...and you have generated a psychodynamic interpretation for oppositional student behavior. Is this cool, or what? Let's try a couple for fun. Suppose you tend to perseverate a lot and just chose 8-8-8. This would yield the term: *"Precocious Intrapsychic Detachment"*. How about 1-3-6 which gets you *"Archetypal Character Sublimation"*. If one description doesn't seem quite right,...don't lose your grin! Just pick three more numbers and create a totally different cryptic term. While you're at it, why not drop a few of these gems at your next parent conference or IEP meeting? And what an ideal way to explain your last chocolate binge? Our crack team of OBM scientists have calculated that you can generate 729 psycho-babble terms from this list. *Let it snow, let it snow, let it snow....*

1. Archetypal	1. Personality	1. Fixation
2. Parataxic	2. Oedipal	2. Orientation
3. Existential	3. Character	3. Cathexis
4. Polymorphous	4. Narcissism	4. Transference
5. Intrusive	5. Mastery	5. Displacement
6. Retentive	6. Fantasy	6. Sublimation
7. Punctuated	7. Object-choice	7. Ambivalence
8. Precocious	8. Intrapsychic	8. Detachment
9. Unconscious	9. Autonomy	9. Striving

Some Personal Favorites:

Go ahead, you're dying to try it out! Make up some lucky numbers. Create a few pet terms and record them below for future snow-blinding interpretations!

_____   _____   _____

_____   _____   _____

_____   _____   _____

Barry T. Christian, Ph.D. (1997)

"Irresistible Future Changes"

While novelty and interest run high and the OBM teacher still holds all the cards, it's easy to move into some convincing predictions about the target student. At this point we like to introduce an element of confusion and curiosity which opens even the iron willed student (who may be feigning disinterest) to some wonderful prognostications. Here are three guidelines for crafting irresistible predictions of future change:

1. Predict irresistible behaviors that are a thinly veiled replica of the ones he *already* performs in a daily habitual manner.

> *"Yes, this stage of adolescent development is always a puzzle. Sometime today...probably not right now but later... you're going to find yourself walking down a crowded hallway somewhere and thinking out loud in your mind about one of the school rules. I don't know which one it will be. At that time, your subconscious mind may tell you something about your profile that could be very useful. Now you've even got me curious as to what you're going to discover. This should really be a fascinating day!"*

> *"This profile seems to suggest you will sometime find yourself starting out with a lot of hope in something, but not finishing. I'm not real sure what all that means ....Maybe like trying to stay out of trouble for a day, but having bad luck...or perhaps trying to get started on some work but getting distracted. I guess we'll just have to wait and find out."*

> *"This is a special profile. There's some indication of restlessness or agitation...that may be displayed in your daily life with episodes of doing the exact opposite of what someone tells you to do....or maybe feeling the need to argue about some issue you really don't even care about. Is it possible that you'll have to follow that demanding life script? This should be a very fascinating day. Let me know what you discover."*

2. Predict behaviors that are *unavoidable* to any student, but which now can be explained as internally driven and purposeful.

> *"Sometime today or this week you're going to find yourself seated, legs stretched out, and resting...even when you don't really feel tired at all.*

When you find yourself in that situation, you may want to listen for any messages your subconscious mind is sending you. This 'seated and resting' thing may be your body's way of slowing you down in order to listen better."

"This profile suggests you may be moving into a period when your thoughts will come so fast that you could say some things without thinking. Later, all this running off at the mouth should make some sense. Maybe we should both listen to see what pops out today?"

3. Predict "either/or" behaviors which are self-fulfilling whether he resists them or performs them.

These are great for setting up the difficult student for your "knowing look" which let's him know you understand his developmental plight. Remember, oppositional kids hate to be understood or "figured out". If you're low-down, mean & rotten, you can also plan for some *control* statements such as "...Hmmm, just as we predicted". I've known stubborn kids who actually refused to perform the predicted misbehaviors, just to keep from hearing those all-knowing comments from the OBM teacher.

"This brief phase of development is always curious to me. Basically, you can expect to find yourself somewhere in the confusion of the school day...and faced with a frozen moment in time where a decision is needed. Everything in your mind will get very clear and focused. Things may go into "slow motion" for just a while. You will then find yourself making some conscious decision to do something important...or resist doing something. Wonder what all that means? Guess we'll just have to wait and find out."

"This is a very unique profile. Seems you'll soon be walking a pathway where your inner drives will demand some kind of positive life changes. Wonder if you will reap all the benefits of those changes...or if some part of you will resist your inner drives? This is often an exciting but confusing stage. It should be educational for both of us to watch how the battle turns out."

As you might guess, the firebreathing oppositional student will actively seek to thwart any simple direct predictions about his behavior. Remember, this is just how they are wired. But also remember that OBM strategies are made to flourish best with this kind of knee-jerk resistance. Any teacher who can come up with the kind of nonsense interpretations discussed earlier should also be more than capable of spinning unavoidable predictions that are equally vague.

Just as an aside, we have sometimes considered whether there should be a 24 hour OBM hotline set up for teachers to call in and get help in crafting outrageous interpretations and predictions. We thought of some catchy numbers such as 1-800-OBM-SAVY. Or, why not a spicy 1-900 number where we give out the same information but add a New Age music background, and charge bigger bucks? Enough already, let's get you set up with the last function of Sigmund Freud in your classroom. Here's the payoff.

Offer A Slick "Behavioral Prescription"

Let's suppose you have already planted the seeds of some wacky profile interpretations. We'll also assume you have choked back some smirks while dropping in an unavoidable or double-bind prediction about near future behavior. Wonderful! Now is your golden opportunity to carry the whole thing to new heights of gleeful absurdity by attaching a helpful therapeutic prescription. After all, what good is that fancy psycho-diagnosis without supportive intervention?

Your prescription is a helpful therapeutic assignment offered to the student as a means of resolving that deep seated intrapsychic conflict. Alternatively, it might be offered quite humbly as a last ditch, desperate means of breaking free from that overwhelming habit or pathologic trait. Well designed behavior prescriptions, offered with a straight face and clinical detachment, allow your oppositional student to resist (as usual!) or comply with equal effectiveness. In fact he can be successful or an abject failure---and still be framed as fully cooperative.

Better yet, the stubborn student who resists your prescription can be cast as the hapless victim of some primitive urge or some developmental need that only the teacher fully understands. Remember, knowledge is power. And, even assumed knowledge carries some clout. Once your prescription has been set in motion, the OBM teacher will earn some days of blissful classroom interactions where "knowing looks" and understanding nods show deep empathy for the student's heroic struggle with "that problem".

Okay, lets think seriously for a moment about a good workable "prescription" for your oppositional student. First off, what's the surest thing you might expect from any suggestion you dream up? That's right: *Resistance!* If a student rushed off and dutifully performed one of my OBM prescriptions, I'd have to seriously doubt whether he was truly oppositional. In reality, these student's are pre-programmed to resist, challenge, and subvert authority. Why should they comply with some silly directive from me, even if it's supposed to help with "that problem"?

Just like our earlier trance inducing predictions about near future behavior, the prescribed treatment for a diagnosed problem must be set up so any behavior (or even non-behavior) is seen as praise-worthy compliance. No matter how the student comes in to class tomorrow, I've got to have some logical reason to smile and congratulate him for his good effort. I've got to take on the persona of myopic Mr. Magoo and "see" some evidence of my student's Herculean effort to work through his problem or forebear under extreme inner pressures. This kid's a hero, no matter what he does!

Let's cut to the chase and look at some helpful OBM prescriptions. For your convenience we are offering three hypothetical scripts on the following pages. It may be necessary to practice these in front of a mirror until you can do them without grinning.

1. For the student who dominates the class by arguing and talking out. Let's assume he has already been given some psycho-babble interpretation of his situation (suppose a 5-3-6, or even a 4-9-7) that has to do with passing through a "critical stage of growth".

"Thanks for stopping by Jim. No doubt you've had more time to think about that interesting personality profile we discussed last week. Isn't it amazing how some thoughts and behaviors can almost be predicted to happen when your psychological development requires them. I've sure noticed some of these things coming out over the past few days. Isn't it great? (The empathetic teacher flashes a grand Ultrabrite smile.) *Remember, this is one of those difficult stages to get through. Some kids get lost in the middle and never seem to find their way out.*

If I could offer only one suggestion during this transition time, it would be this: When confusing thoughts buzz into your head, try to focus your eyes on one nearby object ---something with an earth-tone color---and stare hard at it...until everything in your head settles down. In fact, when you get good at staring, you can even "pretend" to do it in your head while you keep chattering away in class in the usual way. No one needs to know what you're really up to. Well that's just a suggestion. Let me know how things turn out..."

Notice how this prescribed behavior allows for either/or responses. He can stare at an object or just pretend to stare while continuing to talk out as usual. Either way, the OBM teacher has begun to take some implicit control of poor Jim. I can hear you asking, "So when does Jim learn to shut up in class?" Patience grasshopper. First comes the set-up *and then* the sting. Meanwhile, let's look at another common script for an OBM prescription.

2. For the student who argues and mumbles threats under his breath.

"Howdy Mortimer. I just needed a moment or two to say how pleased I was to review your psychological development profile. (Here the teacher may review some of the cryptic findings, or maybe mention some of the recent irresistible behaviors connected with his condition.)

It may be important for you to know that the next couple weeks will be critical in this stage of your development. If you're able to pull all of these free floating thoughts and impulses together at the right time, you'll move easily right into the next stage. I have just one suggestion. During the next couple weeks, you might need to follow your first impulses...like to argue in class or whisper defiant comments under your breath. You might need to follow these impulses from your earlier infantile character structure, even if they do cost you some punishment or peer ridicule. You might even do more than these childhood impulses would demand, just to get through the transition!

I know it will be a struggle and you may have kids thinking you're a jerk or something....But it will be well worth the pain and punishments, don't you think? Of course, you might beat all the odds and move suddenly and effortlessly into the more advanced stage without wrestling with all those impulses. You might find yourself quietly sitting in your desk and working away with no stress at all. Well, either way, I'll be watching to see how the next weeks go. It should be a very interesting study in developmental psychology!"

3. For the hard core resistor, who can't even play the game.

For the rigid kid who can't fathom any impending developmental changes, and knows only to blindly resist all suggestions, we have the following sample presentation. This is a helpful prescription, but quite impossible for anyone to follow. (and that's the idea).

"Greetings Dominic. I'll bet you haven't had a chance to think about that developmental crisis stuff. That situation we discussed may look scary, even impossible. Maybe so, but desperate times require desperate action. There just may be a way to get through this stage and into some peace and quiet...but it's not going to be easy. In fact, I don't know if you can pull it off. If you're ever going to tame those deep impulses and anxieties in your head you're going to have to fight on their turf. You're going to have to deprive your mind of sleep...maybe just survive on two or three hours a night...and you're going to have to start occupying your mind by counting all kinds of strange things, like tiles in the floor, cracks in the sidewalk, lockers in the hallway,....you know what kind of stuff I'm talking about.

You'll have to slave your mind to some intense task in order to wear down those impulses...maybe even have to start counting more and more things like the number of steps you take in a day, ...or the number of breaths you take in a week, or even how many times you swallow during a meal....until you are able to break free and make it into the next peaceful stage. I've even heard of kids in your situation who wore a thick rubber band on their wrist and gave themselves a snap after every two steps they took ...all day long. Well, it's a major move that you're facing here. Let me know what you plan to do...."

If this oppositional kid is really worth his salt, he'll flatly reject the ordeal, but there will also be the sense that he backed down from the OBM teacher's prescription. The idea is to beat this student to the proverbial punch by describing an impossible task that he could never really accomplish (and then let him reject it). After the set up, the teacher may then conclude with: *"I know it's tough...I just wish we could think of some easier way".*

Let's linger a moment at the third script. After throwing down the gauntlet, just let your impossible student simmer a few more days on the back burner. From time to time the teacher may mention the unavoidable behaviors that must continue to be the tell tale symptoms of his latent developmental crisis. Of course these "unavoidable symptoms" are not too different from the daily disruptions the teacher has already endured for most of the school year. But now the teacher is an empathetic diagnostician who can lament the plight of the suffering pre-adolescent (even if he doesn't want his plight lamented!) End up with something like:

> *"It's going to be quite a roller coaster ride.....with no breaks. Meanwhile, just brace yourself the best you can. You can expect a lot more of these powerful impulses, and wild urges, and free floating anxieties......You know what I mean, like making bad decisions, or having some problem words slip out at the wrong times..."*

This entire last scenario is offered as one of the tough cases. Perhaps the best outcome is preserving the teacher's power position in the face-to-face relationship. The teacher continues to have "deeper insights" than the student would like her to have, and the whole resistance routine is now reframed as a relentless struggle...that is the student's personal crisis. Think about it. By diagnosing a developmental crisis, the teacher has actually transformed her oppositional headache student into an emotional cripple who needs understanding and support. The OBM teacher can now get real busy hovering over the bewildered student with excessive controlling "smother love". We all know this as a power trip in some families (so why not use it strategically in the classroom?). There you go smiling again.

Anyway,....if things mellow out in the weeks ahead, the teacher might announce that she had a brainstorm and came up with some easier way for the poor student to crash through that developmental barrier. She might then suggest that he try making a tight fist and squeezing the blood out of his hand (and back up to his brain) whenever stupid urges are detected. This easier prescription would also allow the teacher to continue the psychoanalytic interpretations and be a supportive guide to the student. And look who keeps the power!

But Can It Fly, Wilbur?

If you've lasted this long, you've earned the right to some closure on "Playing Sigmund Freud" in the classroom. Just how do we pull all this slick talk together into a workable OBM strategy? So glad you asked.

Sigmund Freud Method: *(....in a nutshell)*

For your mental processing convenience,
here's a summary of those wild OBM steps:

1. Dream up some sophisticated life transition crisis (remember, psychoanalysis is a fertile field to dig up all manner of developmental problems). It might even help to administer our **Polymorphous Adolescent Development Test** (or just gather up some odd bits of information), display your "data" on a homemade profile chart, and assign a diagnostic term from the **Psycho-Babble Verbiage Generator**.

2. Strengthen your sage-like credibility by predicting some irresistible behaviors or "symptoms" that the student can expect to encounter as he wrestles with his raging developmental crisis. These predictions should be thinly veiled replicas of his current disgusting misbehaviors, or a trance-like preoccupation on mundane daily experiences, including sneaky double bind predictions. You might want to stumble back through the chapter and review these.

3. In a follow-up meeting, offer a behavioral prescription designed to help the student transition through this difficult stage of development. Generally, the prescription *requires* the oppositional student to keep doing a problem behavior---but in a slightly different way from it's "raw form".

4. The diagnosis and prescription should cast the teacher as a wise and helpful observer who is just trying to help the student through a developmental crisis. There should be no hint of antagonism or jockeying for control.

5. The prescribed transition behaviors might include both public and private efforts. If the student resists the outward behaviors, the teacher can still infer that much private mental effort is being expended (and therefore give liberal amounts of daily praise and support for all that internal work).

6. If blatant defiance and resistance are expected from the student, the first prescription should be an impossible task or some extreme ordeal as "the only way out for you". The supportive OBM teacher should then commiserate with the student and lament his plight (i.e., "you're really stuck at this impasse...I wish the solution were easier"). The teacher can either enjoy helping the cripple she has created, or later offer an easier prescription.

7. Once any compliance is established, begin to let the next prescribed behaviors "drift" toward more benign (i.e., tolerable) symptoms. There is an art form to this. Spend some time window shopping our *Subtle Transformations* in Appendix III.

Chapter Seven

Practice Tantrum Sessions
Do them right, or not at all

Terrorist Demands And Negative Reinforcement

Here's a good one for explosive elementary kids who are preparing themselves for major conduct problems in mid school. We're talking about the resistant and defiant students who punish their teacher with red-faced screaming and kicking fits. These are always entertaining to watch in someone else's classroom. Perhaps unknown to these local resistance fighters, the technical term for their control strategy is "negative reinforcement". That is, they are willing to terminate an aversive stimulus (i.e., their tantrum) as a means of reinforcing the teacher for complying with their demands. Sounds like those demanding terrorists who threaten to blow up the airliner. You may also recall seeing this negative reinforcement strategy practiced by tearful children with loud voices and reaching hands, at the Wal-Mart check out displays. As usual, there are many settings for the same strategy.

Quick And Powerful Intervention

Let's be practical. A first line of intervention to any of these situations might be the simple application of direct authority: "Yo, Listen up! Stop doing that and do this instead." As pointed out in Chapter One, why use some multi-step intervention when you have total control and overwhelming decisive power? The fact of life is, we often have far less raw power in the classroom than we think. Besides, when we call in a major air strike against these classroom terrorists, they'll just take hostages somewhere else. Instead, try to think of the OBM teacher as a highly trained "lone commando"---maybe like Rambo, Chuck Norris or Ophra. This respected but somewhat uncommon teacher must go in on a special mission where other teachers, counselors, and principals have failed. She must get in, make radical changes in the student's behavior, and then get out before he even knows what happened.

Good News For Tantrum Sufferers!

We have found that the assignment of OBM "practice tantrum sessions" has generated quick (almost immediate) deceleration of this problematic behavior These little sessions have also enhanced the teacher's sense of confidence, and have even preserved the student-teacher relationship. As usual, this slick strategy avoids any heated confrontations with the terrorist Kindergartner or the hostage taking second grader. You may recall the Israeli government policy: "We don't negotiate with terrorists". Well, rather than confront or negotiate, the OBM teacher embarks on a course of supportive "training" for stress management. Try to imagine the Delta Force serving sandwiches and cokes to those bad-attitude terrorists, and then getting all concerned that these sociopaths haven't been receiving proper rest and exercise. Maybe that's just a mite far fetched, but the "benign concern" principle still holds. Read on.

I was consulting in a small K through 12 school in an isolated high desert community where you would expect to find an abundance of harmony and tranquillity. Not so. A new teacher at that school was about ready to surrender and seek out more peaceful work at a prison or trauma center. Her career doubts were due to one extremely disruptive 3rd grader who was virtually holding the classroom hostage with daily tantrums. After observing only one of little Anthony's fits, I was already considering residential treatment options. This kid rejected any imposed structure (e.g., "do this worksheet") and would flash into sudden violent tantrums where he would dump work materials, tear up his paper, and violently throw himself on the floor kicking and crying. Anthony also had a habit of screaming "I hate you, I hate you all!" at the top of his lungs, while barricading himself under a table (i.e., where you couldn't reach him!), and even doing some pseudo-psychotic head banging if he had an audience.

Our Clinical Studies Show....

After only about one week, Anthony's daily tantrums had been totally extinguished and he was freed up to develop some more civilized means of resistance. Our neophyte teacher was one of those OBM naturals who received only a few minutes of consultation on the "practice tantrums" idea and promptly set about to change a student's life. Below are the general steps that have been repeatedly applied in school settings:

How To Do The "Practice Tantrums" Intervention

1. Reframe The Problem:

Instead of focusing on Anthony's resistance and tantrums, the teacher expressed concern that this student had "too much pressure inside" just like a shaken bottle of Cherry Cola.   Of course, all that pressurization was responsible for the explosive episodes (An idea ripped off from Chapter Six?). The teacher might also have gone on to declare that little Anthony "was being too hard or demanding on himself" (Chapter Four, item 2). This would have introduced even more empathetic concern.

2. Prescribe The Solution:

Whenever there is too much pressure somewhere, it's a good idea to "turn the cap slowly" to gain some controlled "release" for that pressure. The teacher's explanation to Anthony was that she would allow him "pressure release" practice time each day for one full week. Since it seemed there were already some behaviors that worked for him (i.e., the tantrums); why not use them to help the problem? Anthony was told he would be given some practice tantrum sessions each day.

3. Design The Curriculum:

The teacher sat down with a ruler and felt tip marker, and worked out a weekly practice schedule. This grid listed several necessary practice behaviors which were slightly weakened versions of the real thing:

Making and holding a mean facial expression, tearing up a piece of junk mail and throwing it all forcefully in a waste basket, (while) screaming "I hate you" in a loud voice ten times; (next) lying on the floor and kicking a cement block wall ten times; and then sitting under a work table and hitting himself on the head with a rolled up piece of newspaper while crying out like there was real pain. (Sounds like a punk rock concert to me.)

Anyway, for each target behavior, Anthony would receive an evaluation (and point credits) according to how "real" his performance looked. There was even the offer of some bonus points if he could add a little something extra or spicy into the practice behaviors!   At the end of the week his points would be tallied and he could use them to purchase some fantastic reward (well, sort of). The whole program could be extended for additional days if more "pressure" needed to be released.

4. Operate The Program:

As part of his next counseling session, the teacher and I arranged for the regular classroom to be empty and invited Anthony to the "planning session". After reviewing his need for a pressure release, we explained the target behaviors and briefly demonstrated each one. We then had bewildered Anthony role play one entire practice tantrum! Some of his efforts were heartily praised while others were critiqued. Anthony was also reminded of the reward he might be able to earn. We even hired veteran game show announcer, Don Pardo, to remind our player of all those fabulous prizes he might win. (not)

During the following week, Anthony reluctantly practiced his tantrums during part of the morning recess period. Almost magically, his "real" tantrums declined on the first day. By the time I arrived for the next class visit and counseling session, Anthony had performed no real tantrums that entire day and was *refusing* to do his practice session. Despite the OBM teacher's theatrical coaching, our target student was also getting a bit sloppy in his earlier practice sessions.

5. Terminate The Program With An "Open Door" For Future Needs:

Somewhere in the middle of the first week, Anthony began to resist doing his practice tantrums. *(Note: He claimed that they looked foolish!)*. The OBM teacher feigned some concern that the pressure release might fail if not carried out properly for the full week. She then made a private deal with Anthony to allow him to skip his regular practice sessions if he didn't feel "in the mood" and would rather just go out to recess. However, in exchange, he would be willing to do some "excellent" practicing in the regular class setting if the right kind of mood came over him. The teacher worked out a secret signal (Remember Chapter Two?) for Anthony to give her if he felt the urge to do some tantrum "practicing" (i.e., it was decided that whenever Anthony began to look upset, angry, or nervous; he would be given some immediate pressure release practice.)

Long Term "Recovery Work" For The Ex-Tantrumer

This termination is really smooth. But we can all agree that "old habits die slowly" and it's just a matter of time before good ol' Anthony gets the itch to tantrum again. When this actually happened several days later, our OBM teacher just pulled out the clipboard with the evaluation grid. She quietly approached Anthony and encouraged him to "do a really excellent job on this one" so he could earn the maximum credits for each behavior. Interestingly, the teacher also coached Anthony to make sure he was "really in the mood" before attempting a classroom tantrum. If the mood wasn't full blown, it was suggested that he delay the tantrum until he could do it justice.

One Day At A Time

As luck would have it, I walked into the classroom sometime later and found Anthony backslidden to his old ways. He was under the table again and the teacher was looking for the clipboard. I peeked under the table and asked if he was in the mood to do a "serious" tantrum. In his own oppositional manner, Anthony shouted "No!" and returned to thumping the back of his head against the table leg. I agreed with him . *"You're right about that. You're still in too good a mood for this. Do you want to wait,...or just go ahead and try one anyway?"* He still said nothing, but just sat there with a grim contorted expression. I waited a while and then added: *"The teacher can still give you a couple of points even if it's just a wimp practice job,...but we've got to get it done now, before the bell."* Poor Anthony kicked out at a table leg, folded his arms across his chest, and slumped back against the wall.

This kid was still deep down stubborn and oppositional, but that day he came to see himself as a tantruming has-been,...totally washed up as a classroom tyrant. Frankly, he was now an eight year old failure in the fit-throwing business. I guess all that pressure got leaked out somehow. Anyway, Anthony refused to talk. We suggested that he just sit there under the table for awhile and try to work up an angry mood. The class returned to other matters. Some minutes later the bell rang and Anthony climbed out from under the table and lined up for the cafeteria. We thought this might be a real good time to use "planned ignoring". It was.

In follow up consultations with the OBM teacher I learned that Anthony was nominally compliant during the remainder of the semester. Our rookie teacher was smiling again and back in control of the classroom. To my knowledge she never turned in her Peace Corps application, and may still be teaching in some blissful desert community. Below are a few suggestions left with this heroic educator for maintaining Anthony's gains.

82

Modifications For The Practice Tantrums Strategy:

1. **Daily Prognostications And Friendly Wagers:**
In the morning, ask the student to make a prediction as to whether he will "get in the mood" sometime during the day for a good spontaneous practice session. The teacher might suggest a friendly wager, and always bet against the student's prediction.

2. **Audio Tapes:**
Inform the student that you intend to audio tape his next efforts at practicing a spontaneous tantrum in class. You might pave the way by also taping some of his private practice sessions during recess. These tapes can be reviewed and further critiqued in a future coaching session. Some of the "classics" can also be sent home and the parent asked to rate how "real" the episode sounded! Think about how much fun you could have with some good video taped episodes. You might even send one in to *America's Funniest Home Videos*. Better yet, save some videos until your oppositional student grows up, becomes a highly visible political figure, and might be motivated to buy them back. Of course, there's also a good chance he might grow up to become a Mafia leader. (This could make the sell back negotiations much more delicate.)

3. **Peer Review Panel:**
Assemble a panel of classmates to observe a demonstration tantrum and vote on whether it should earn any credits for authenticity. I have sometimes used a simple show of hands vote right in the classroom.

4. **Peer Demonstration Role-Plays:**
During the introductory phase, ask one or more peers to role play how the target student typically "does" his tantrum thing. This may be even more revealing than a teacher demonstration. Ask the oppositional student to comment on how well the other classmates were able to capture the true style and essence of his tantrums. As usual, the teacher should avoid any spells of hysterical laughter.

5. Tantrum Permits:

Check out Chapter 11 for some hints on how to sell time-limited permits for "doing" classroom disruptions. These flashy permits also make great stocking stuffers and party favors!

Final Thought: Any time you have a student who throws honest-to-goodness temper tantrums, you have a brittle and vulnerable child. Such a student is crying out for limits and security. This is a great place to start your OBM career! Just to help get things rolling, you'll find a sample Practice Tantrums evaluation chart on the following page.

Practice Tantrums

Barry T. Christian, Ph.D. (1997)

Child's Name: _____

Practice Location: _____

Practice Times: _____

Tantrum Behaviors	Mon	Tue	Wed	Thr	Fri
1. _____					
2. _____					
3. _____					
4. _____					
5. _____					
6. _____					

Daily Rating Codes:

S = 10 points: Satisfactory (looks and sounds real!)

S- = 5 points: Wimpy But Acceptable

U = 0 points: Unsatisfactory (totally unbelievable performance)

Rewards:

Penalties:

Chapter Eight

Zero Tolerance and the "Gotcha! Game"

Our present chapter deals with an entire group of students..."the difficult class". Not one, but a bunch of wise-achers. We've used this one at home with the kids; I've assigned it in family therapy; and a few brave OBM teachers have also had some fun with it. Suppose you are dealing with a mildly annoying behavior. Something less depraved than drive-by milkshake throwing but more serious than, say, classroom hiccups. Within that vast range of irritation are many potential target behaviors emitted daily by our oppositional students. Hmm...What to do ...what to do...

Problems With Consistency

Major disruptions command our attention, but those lessor irritants slip in and out of awareness like a mentally challenged mosquito in the RV. Only when we get buzzed again do we remember how very much we are bothered. Only when we are having our own bad hair day do we vow vengeance on such disgusting classroom behaviors. These stressful times allow us to reach some fully paranoid conclusions: Most assuredly, those students who cultivate such repertoires of vile little quirks are also the same caste of self-willed individuals bent on seizing control! We declare total war on nail biting, pencil tapping, messy desks, or those getting-the-last-word addicts. ...Ah, but then tomorrow comes and the grass is growing and the birds are tweeting, and it's payday. We call a truce with the mild aggravations of the classroom and let them drone on in peace. And so it goes until that headache returns.

Values Clarification

One response to the roller coaster of tolerance and irritation is to conduct a quick values clarification. What's important to me? What's worth the energy of confrontation? How much can I live with as a semi-rational person? Is Weird Harold's tall tale telling a genuine disruption to the learning process? Do Ernie's unsolicited sick comments trample on class policy? You might want to take a quick gander at Appendix II as you consider when to draw the line in the sand and declare "enough is enough".

When you decide that some bothersome student behavior is your own "issue", then simply let it go. In fact, you might want to box up all your "personal issues" and Fed Ex them to John Bradshaw. Alternatively, when you are convinced that certain behaviors are beyond normal toleration *(i.e., ------insert your own neurotic example here----------)*, then you might be ready to make your formal declaration of Zero Tolerance (ZT). During the course of developing this OBM strategy, we concluded that those minor high frequency behaviors were often a blemish on the classroom program.

Because this particular strategy was aimed at unwanted but highly visible irritations, it was proposed that we code our procedure as the ZIT Program (Zero Infraction Tolerance). To make a long story bearable, our first public use of the ZIT treatment methods generated a massive outcry from the Association of Cosmetically Challenged National Educators. We were virtually forced to modify the name to it's present form.

Zero Tolerance:

Remember those *Miami Vice* guys waging war on the Colombian drug lords? Back then, I recall some effort to establish a zero tolerance drug policy for all incoming vessels and vehicles. As I understand it, the deal was that *any amount* of illegal drugs discovered on a yacht or plane could result in immediate seizure of that fancy piece of hardware. The intended message was: Don't bring any of that stuff to our shores. Small amounts would be treated as large amounts. No warnings or second chances would be given. Monitoring and enforcement would be consistent, and penalties would be handed down like predictable clockwork. You know this idea was too rational and simple to last very long. But if it had, we can bet there would have been some serious behavior modification at all levels of the pecking order.

Teachers who use Zero Tolerance declarations almost always make waves, take heat, and usually live to see changes in class behavior. In fact, there are local school buildings where certain disruptive behaviors are routinely winked at in all classrooms except one. Somewhere, there is that one teacher who tenaciously defends a personal policy which prohibits "gross behavior X". Student's navigate through the day and automatically delete that one behavior in only classroom. Now *that's* discrimination learning. Below are some items to consider when selecting a ZT policy:

1. **Choose worthy target behaviors:**

As always, you should submit the intended target behavior to personal tests of practicality. You might want to look over the list of probing questions provided in Appendix II.

2. **Consider alternative interventions:**

Even worthy target behaviors may not be appropriate for this particular strategy. Hopefully we have convinced you that there are dozens of creative strategies for managing oppositional behavior.

3. **Select behaviors that can't be easily disputed:**

This gets back to the old "observability" requirement when you used to be more conscientious in writing your instructional objectives. A ZT policy for "bad attitude" would most likely result in endless arguments and self-justification speeches ---especially from our oppositional students. Because there will always be some room for argument, apply the "rational person" test. If a panel of "rational observers" were to witness the act, would they agree it had occurred? Perhaps you might locate some of these rational-type observers in your classroom? I personally like the "dictator observer" test which gives the teacher the power of an NFL referee (before the video replay days).

4. **Select behaviors that are a chronic nuisance:**

Sure, we should already expect ZT on sinister felony acts (e.g., hot-wiring the principal's '65 VW Bus for a lunch time joy ride, or sending out fake termination letters to the entire faculty); but the policy actually seems to work best when aimed at lesser offenses (e.g., using certain reflexive "put downs" in class).

5. **Select consequences that are fully controlled by the teacher:**

As we've heard from venerated sages of the teacher's lounge, *"Don't make threats that you can't deliver"*. Ideally, the consequence should be unavoidable, assigned immediately, and the teacher should have easy access to them (e.g., loss of one point from a behavior chart, assigned one minute increments of recess delay, confiscation of some ordinary school work item, etc.) We've had good luck with response cost token economies where one "ticket" is fined per display of the ZT target behavior. Keep your penalties simple and convenient.

6. **Consequences should be mild and repeatable:**

Because we are suggesting target behaviors with a moderate frequency type target behaviors (e.g., chair squeaking, social etiquette foibles, forgetting key tasks, selected gross acts, etc.) it will be important to have designated consequences that can be repeated two hundred times a day if needed. They should allow the student to remain engaged in learning, and cause little disrupt the learning process. A rule of thumb might be that a good consequence should not require more than 10 seconds of teacher time (e.g., making a statement, gesturing toward the student, marking on a lesson book, placing a tally mark on a chart, etc.)

Remember, these mild consequences are not intended to cause great pain or isolation from society. Rather, I see them as a "response interruption", just enough to momentarily stop the behavior, let the student know he was caught, and provide for an easy "reset button" so he can start over. As you might guess, I have some personal OBM-type favorites.

As a teacher-friendly assigned consequence, I like to require that the policy violator close his eyes and count *"out loud in your head"* to any number above 15. (If he feels particularly penitent, he can mentally count to some higher number.) This seems to be less disruptive to the class routine than our old consequence of requiring the violator to stand on his left foot and clap his hands over head ten times.

As another mild-immediate-repeatable consequence, I require the student to close his eyes and imagine having a large messy banana cream pie pushed into his face. For a repeat offender who doesn't seem to profit from experience, I might have him close his eyes and imagine having a cold bucket of water thrown on him, falling into an ice water dunk tank, or picturing himself getting sick in the cafeteria and vomiting all over his clothes. The best thing about these consequences is the shock effect, without all that clean up work.

Getting Started With Your Zero Tolerance Policy:

It's basically simple. Once you have your ducks in a row, call a formal class meeting. Some teachers may prefer to enlist a student as the old English "town crier" who walks around the classroom in period costume doing the "Hear ye, Hear ye" routine. Personally, I worry about teachers who go that far to call a meeting. Anyway, explain to the class that an important new policy will soon go into effect regarding your pet peeve behavior. Be prepared to demonstrate the exact disgusting behavior in question (along with any suggested substitute behavior). Also demonstrate how your swift but mild consequence will be meted out *for each and every violation.*

Sneaky Trick #1:
Introduce the ZT policy as a short-term trial (e.g., for the rest of the week) rather than for ever and ever. You can always extend, modify, or terminate the policy at the end of the trial period. Isn't that what they do with temporary taxes, surcharges, and mill levy scams?

Sneaky Trick #2:
Because your ZT policy is aimed at some chronic but mild misbehavior, take the liberty of adding "arbitrary and capricious" methods of evaluation that legitimize your lighthearted dictatorial powers. To cut through the whining and chatter, announce that the decision to fine violators will lean to the strict and "impossible to please" side (i.e., *"If I see it, hear it, or even imagine it, you're dead meat. Period."*).

Sneaky Trick #3:
Rather than ending with a pep talk and some pedantic encouragement to avoid the annoying little behavior in question, why not do the opposite? Wear a badge-a-minute button that grimly states: MAKE MY DAY. Encourage students to "get sloppy" and "take the fall" as early casualties of the ZT policy.

Okay, enough abstraction. Below is some sample rhetoric to get you into the concrete:

Zero Tolerance Script

(The OBM teacher is standing before the class prepared to show the ZT notice. The bold information looks something a kin to an Old West "Wanted" poster. There is an ominous pointing finger, and the whole thing might be printed on some wild neon pink card stock.) Is that concrete enough? The OBM teacher might give an inspiring presentation such as is outlined below:

"Class, I've always believed that Language Arts is an exciting adventure in learning. It truly deserves our respect (yak, yak, yak).... Therefore, I'm beginning a new policy which will be strictly enforced through next Friday. The next time I introduce our assignment for the day, there will be no groaning, mournful sighs, or cute hissy fits. If I hear any of these things, ...or even if you do something that remotely suggests to me you're unhappy, you'll win a helpful reminder. For each violation, you will earn yourself 30 seconds waiting after class so you can meditate on the joy of learning. This is a Zero Tolerance policy which means no warnings or second chances. (The teacher holds up the colorful poster for all to see and then staples it to a corkboard.)

Now, just between us, I'm expecting I'll need to monitor at least a half dozen students after class. These are the kids who will be meditating while everyone else splits for lunch. If you feel lucky, go ahead and plan a good moan when we move into our lesson... (long pause)...Well, hey gang. Guess what? It's time once again for Language Arts! Take out your text book and your work book. Turn to Chapter 7 in the textbook which is on page 104. (The teacher intently and deliberately scans the class for any thinly veiled signs of unhappiness, and "awards" 30 second meditation opportunities where needed.)

NOTICE:
There Will Be
ZERO
TOLERANCE

For This Behavior:

_____

During These Dates:
_____

With Immediate & Appropriate
Consequences For All Violations.

Double Your Fun: Add the "Gotcha! Game"

When a rational educator first thinks of a "Gotcha! Game" in the classroom, what expectations come to mind? Basically, you might expect that the teacher would stay alert to target behavior violations among the students. Whenever one was observed (as with the ZT policy), the teacher would approach the student, announce "Gotcha!", and give some reasonable consequence. This was basically what you had expected, right? Well, not even...

Ahhh, this is *Outrageous B-Mod* and so there's always some delightful twist to the standard methods. The Gotcha! Game is a reverse strategy which places the students in charge of monitoring the *teacher's* compliance.   In our above ZT contingency, the teacher has implicitly promised to be diligent in scanning the class and responding to negative behaviors. So, who evaluates the teacher? That's right, *the students are now given the assignment of monitoring the teacher's compliance* with the ZT contingency. They are now charged with assigning penalties to the teacher if she gets soft hearted or goes simple. True, the students must still comply with the ZT policy, but now the teacher is also put on the spot,   and required to nab all those violators.

Whenever the teacher blatantly overlooks a whine or moan in Language Arts class, a feisty student (probably Oppositional Eddy, himself) will point a bony ET finger at her and announce: "Gotcha!". When caught in the act of slacking off, the teacher agrees to accept a penalty.   When I used to assign this little exercise in family therapy, a favorite penalty was to have the offending parent stand on a chair and sing a song requested by the child. The Gotcha game is intended to keep everybody sharp. No wonder it's set up with a time limit.

Potential Penalties For The Teacher:

You'll remember gag penalties like having celebrities take a chance seated over the dunk tank, or having the university president kiss a pig. We've even heard some old timer's promise to eat their hat. What could a teacher offer as a self-penalty for missing an obvious student ZT violation?   In order to protect our OBM teachers, we have not mentioned this little matter on the sample Rules Poster (at the end of the chapter). You should consider some self-penalties anyway. While it might be more fun to survey the class, or turn the whole question into an essay assignment, we have taken the liberty to suggest just a few penalties for the teacher:

Do an impromptu impression of that uptight teacher across the hall "having a bad day".

Offer the class a 20 second demonstration of how she herself might have looked in this grade---doing the same ZT target behavior.

Award a wacky behavior permit (check out Chapter 11) or a credit coupon to the student who first gave her the Gotcha! signal. See the sample class rules poster and credit coupon at the end of this chapter.

Give a Bonus Point voucher slip that may be attached to either a homework paper or the next unit examination.

(In a situation where the Gotcha Game seems to be generating a lot of interest and participation) Jot down the initials of each responding student, place them all in a jar, and hold a daily drawing for your offbeat reward.

(In times of austerity and budget constraints) Have the first responding Gotcha! student stand by his desk and receive a rousing applause from the in-house audience. You might even play a tape recording of the *Pomp and Circumstance* musical score as a back drop for that thunderous applause.

Don't Run It Into The Ground:

Try to picture yourself playing that arcade game where you have a bright yellow nerf club and must clobber elf noggins as they pop up and surprise you. You hammer one and another pops up, and on and on it goes until your quarter is spent. In a similar way, we have found it takes about two weeks of ZT consequences to stamp out a chronic nuisance behavior. Once that particular behavior isn't a big issue anymore, why not just quietly drop the ZT policy? Always get rid of a program before it turns mundane and boring. If it really did something for you, try substituting another annoying behavior and changing some of the consequences. No matter how things turn out, it's always a good idea to keep your yellow nerf club handy.

Check out the following pages for some sample forms and support materials. These are not as wonderful as the gems your own classroom committee might produce!

Gotcha! Game
Official Class Rules Poster

1. These rules are intended to help the teacher remember to strictly enforce the Zero Tolerance policy in our classroom. It's simple. Each time a violation happens in class, the teacher gives a penalty. There are no exceptions.

Target Behavior:

_____

2. Any time the teacher, Ms./Mr._____, forgets to enforce the above Zero Tolerance rule, the student who observes it should immediately:

> ***A. Face the teacher***
> ***B. Point an index finger at the teacher***
> ***C. Say: "Gotcha!"***
> ***D. Tell the teacher about the violation***

3. If the teacher, or a majority vote of the class (either one) agrees that a violation was missed, the first Gotcha! student will be awarded one Credit Coupon that may be saved for purchasing fabulous prizes and benefits in the class.

4. Any student who claims to see a Zero Tolerance violation and says Gotcha! to the teacher, when no real violation occurred (by teacher judgment or class majority vote) will be given the same regular penalty that would be assigned for a rule violation.

5. Other Rules:

Barry T. Christian, Ph.D. (1997)

You forgot to enforce a **Zero Tolerance** rule!

Gotcha! Game

****

CREDIT COUPON

****

THIS COUPON WORTH

10

CREDITS

Save For Fabulous Prizes & Benefits

Chapter Nine

Paradoxic Restraint from Positive Changes

What happens when you try to encourage an oppositional student to improve his attitude, or behavior? That's right! You get knee-jerk resistance. Okay, then what happens if you just sit down with the oppositional student and try to convince him through logical argument that he needs to get with the program? Correct again. You get more knee-jerk resistance. Well then, what happens if you fall down on one knee, clasp your hands together, and plead with the student to change his ways? Also Correct. You get both uncontrolled laughter *and* knee-jerk resistance. Notice any recurring theme here? These kids are programmed at the factory to resist, obstruct, and dispute. Why do we keep expecting that the old standard warnings and lecture methods will reach them?

Warning of Negative Outcomes:

Hopefully we've learned something here. With these kids, we need to work smarter, not harder (see Chapter One, OBM assumption #2). Often when I see an oppositional student having a semi-good day, it becomes an opening for paradoxic restraint. I have a brief visit with the student and try to establish a coach-to-player kind of atmosphere. While maintaining a rather serious demeanor, I express concern that there may be a down side to improved behavior at school. In fact, this student might just as well be warned that rapid behavioral improvements can generate a host of negative outcomes. This announcement usually gets his attention and then I follow up with *"...and I'm only telling you this for your own good."* This kind of phrase is usually good for getting his ears perked up and pushing him to find something to resist. Remember OBM Principle #3: Confusion is almost as good as compliance.

Let's pause here for just a second and reconsider the psychological profile we have established for this oppositional student. It's like one of those basic immutable laws of physics: Any pull in one direction will tend to generate an equal and opposite pull in the other direction. Is this pretty close? Rather than patting him on the back and kindly saying *"Thanks for selling out to the proper hierarchy of authority, and finally embracing the established goals of education"*, I try to artfully do the opposite. When you apply this paradoxic restraint method, remember that any sign of patronizing condescension or even the slightest smirk on your face will shoot a hole in the bottom of your canoe!

Problems With Success

Suppose you just won the $10,000,000 that Ed McMahan has been promising you for years. If we really pushed ourselves, we might be able to generate a list of actual problems that could come with your good fortune (e.g., big taxes, con artists, decadence, sudden magnification of all your smallest moral defects, new found stupidity, etc.). In the same way, the present intervention gives you the job of brainstorming some plausible problems that could result if your stubborn little classroom buddy decided to straighten out and fly right.

I have actually used some of the items below with impressionable mid-school bad guys. Please note that each "problem" is actually a hidden benefit that is deliberately presented as negative. Also, be aware that a good discussion of this list tends to induce a light trance state as the student drifts in and out of his imagination and "tries on" your fantasy land predictions. Smooth, very smooth. Now put yourself in wild Willie's place. Suppose, for some reason, he has just completed two days of fairly decent classroom performance. You have noticed his modest trend toward acceptable behavior and stage a brief visit to strategically restrain any future progress. We hope you will enjoy the sample OBM scripts below:

You Better Watch Out For This "Success" Stuff Because:

1."A lot of your old "bad news" friends may drift away from you. They may even get into some serious trouble on their own, without you being anywhere around. You may be the last to know what happened when you hear they got busted for something. The police may not even consider you as part of their group anymore. Hey, that's like being totally forgotten..."

2. *"As you improve more and more at school, think of how you're going to handle it when people start to bug you to join their clubs and activities. What about when the coaches and faculty sponsors start to invite you out for sports. Might as well kiss all your free time goodbye. What a bummer."*

3. *"Think of your new reputation and all those new friends starting to like you. It can be a real drag. It can also take a lot of energy to walk down the hallway every day and have to say Hi back to so many other students. Sometimes you'll wish all those kids didn't like you ....just to get some peace and quiet."*

4. *"I've heard of some kids like you who have improved too quickly, and got really embarrassed when teachers started liking them. You know, like waving, saying Hi, joking around with you in class. If you're not used to it, that kind of teacher attention can be real difficult."*

5. *"I've also known guys like you who insisted on too much school improvement. The next thing they knew, a lot of nice looking girls started to notice them. One fellow started getting notes in his locker from two different girls at the same time....and that led to all kinds of problems. You really have to be aware of the stress that can happen if you keep going like you are."*

6. *" You know, there's probably a lot of things you enjoy right now that you'll have to give up as this behavior improvement stuff continues. Think of all the free time those guys have on their hands when they drop out of school or get kicked out. All day long they can just sit alone at home and watch soaps and game shows, while hundreds of other kids have to be here together at school.*

7. *Think of it. If you quit school early, you could even get a head start on finding some kind of a minimum wage job...and just settle into it for life. Everyone else would have to wait till they graduated or went to college. You could earn maybe several hundred bucks---before all the other kids graduate with their fancy diplomas. Might even save enough to buy some old car, fix it up, and then try to keep it running for the rest of your adult life. Who says you have to graduate to make good money? As long as you're happy with fewer things, you don't need to earn as much as all your friends who graduate.*

8. You've got to think of 'life style quality'. Don't let peer pressure force you to stay in school when you can drop out and really 'be somebody' special. Yes, I can tell you've got a lot to think about before you get all caught up in some kind of new self-improvement and personal success behavior."

9. "By the way, have you thought what too much improvement (too quickly) could do to your parents at home? All these sudden changes might be too much for your dear old mom to bear. She doesn't have a heart condition and anything, does she? I've heard of parents who had kids improve too quickly....They get some kind of nervous spells...I think they call them anxiety attacks...That's what can happen if parents aren't prepared. You need to go very slow. Have you given any kind of warning to your parents? Can you imagine the kind of confusion they might have as they talk about all your new improvements when you're not around? What are they supposed to say to all the neighbors, and the other family members who are used to hearing about your problems? What about your little sister? Isn't she used to being the only good student in the family? Don't you owe her some kind of warning? We have to consider how she might handle all these changes."

Okay, you get the idea. There are dozens of possible warnings about "too much" or "too sudden" success. Keep in mind that you are planting seeds for future pensive thought. You are literally crafting fantasy daydreams that are ten times more compelling than straight on pedantic lectures. This is especially true with our early adolescent oppositional-defiant students. All the while, you are embedding these (let's call them what they are) "hypnotic suggestions", in everyday language that seems to discourage any positive changes.

How's that stubborn student supposed to resist your ideas? Should he argue back that his old ways were indeed stupid and ineffective? Or should he argue that he's not really worthy of all those fantasy benefits? Is this slick or what? Sometimes our triumphal OBM teachers have to leave the room, find a safe place, and just laugh uncontrollably for a few minutes.

Who Will Be Most Upset?

Oppositional kids also tend to be very competitive. A slightly different way to induce a light trance state is to make leading inquiries about who will be most upset to learn of his forthcoming improvements. As you make inquiries, be aware of how slight shifts in language can help carry the student further into your word pictures. Look back over the past section and notice how I framed the success inquiries in "when you improve" and "as you do better" (i.e., suggesting it's definitely going to happen). There can be a place for "If you do better", but that's usually at the very beginning while you are opening the subject.

Ostensibly we are just making concerned inquiries about the future. At the same time we are also planting those seeds of suggestion----and allowing the oppositional student to make observable, measurable improvements in his school life by resisting our concerns. In the immortal words of Colonel Hannibal Smith, *"I love it when a plan comes together"*.

Check out some of these sample inquiries. Yes, many of them have already gone through our rigorous OBM field testing with oppositional mid schoolers.

1."What about your Math teacher? Isn't he the one who had you busted last week in the office? He might have thought you were a low life who would never amount to anything. How's he going to handle it when all these improvements are connected to your name. That guy might blow a fuse! It's not easy for a faculty member to lose face like that."

2. "Your cousins are those older guys who do real well in cross country. I'll bet they don't even give you the time of day now that they've earned their varsity letter jackets. Will they be upset to hear about your fine reputation here at the mid-school? Of course, It could cause some serious family problems if your parents started bragging about all your new achievements."

3. "Maybe your old buddies will be the most upset to see these improvements. They might be worried that you'll get stuck up and too cool for them. As you get more and more confident, you might even stay in school and graduate. Probably go on to some kind of college; and then get one of those good paying jobs. I'll bet they think you're going to move right out of the old neighborhood. Can you imagine their reaction? I can just see a couple years from now. All your buddy's unemployed, hanging around the old neighborhood, just on the street, talking trash. Here comes Lewis, the local success story, cruising by in a sweet looking fire red Corvette ---tinted windows rolled up, stereo CD playing, and not even looking at them. Yes, you can see why some of these guys might get pretty upset with your new style. Do you think it's really worth all that trouble to keep improving like you are now?.......By the way, have you ever sat in a vette? You just look like the kind of guy who might drive one of those things"

Remember How Self-Conscious You Used To Be?

Keep in mind that our fragile adolescents live out each day performing for an imaginary audience. Often that audience is quite critical. In their private world they are also convinced that they are discovering deep new emotions and profound original ideas---all never before experienced in human history. It's quite normal for an early adolescent to invest a large portion of his waking hours contemplating how he comes across to his peer audience. If you understand this gross ego-centricism, your OBM interventions can be deeper, focused, and more effective. Okay, let's all say it together: *"Work smarter , not harder"*.

Chapter Ten

Divide and Conquer
Strategic Gang-Busting Techniques

Dealing With G. Khan & Associates

It's hard enough dealing with one obstinate student, but sometimes they run in packs. Teachers find that the resistance and cockiness displayed by one lone student can be multiplied when that student is supported by tough guy peers. As a rookie counselor in the schools, I recall trying to venture directly into the well-defended back corner of classrooms to break up rowdy cliques. Just like you, I've also attempted to move desks, make examples, and preach on the dangers of "hanging around with the wrong crowd".

Any conclusions? Probably we've all learned that whatever social glue holds these kids together, is stronger than our feeble efforts with a verbal crowbar. In fact, sometimes my attempt to break up local power blocs has actually given them a rallying point, and helped to strengthen their resolve to stay together (and make my life miserable). I really do believe in working smarter. So now I avoid trying to dous e fire s with the proverbial bucket of unleaded premium.

Strategy #1: Pull The Plug On The Leader

Old Indian saying: "Cut off snake's head and rest of body die soon." Sometimes your difficult students hang together only through the daily maintenance and charisma of a self-proclaimed leader. Actually, this is the easiest scenario for "bloc busting". It requires a mild but methodical plan for separating the leader from his gangster constituents. For those behavior technologists among us, the proper term for this strategy has always been "successive approximations". In our case, the criterion performance is a significant reduction in daily contact between Obstinate Al and his feisty followers.

On the following pages are a few potent strategies to weave into your daily teaching activities:

1. Adopt A Teacher's Pet:
Gradually let everyone discover that the gang leader is one of your personal favorites in class. Not his ruffian cronies, just him only.

2. Selective Blindness:
Generally ignore any of Impossible Al's misbehavior. Better yet, just crack up with laughter at his shenanigans ("Isn't that the cutest thing...yak, yak, gush, yak"). Of course, you will also plan to ignore or discount any similar efforts at humor by his low life associates.

3. Token Gifts And Favors:
Frequently bring in curiosities for the big fella (e.g., newspaper clippings, special interest articles, etc.). Speaking in front of his outcast buddies, ask Al if he would like you to "put in a good word" for him with some of his other teachers. Mention that you've already given him some good press.

4. Blame Others:
Whenever Mr. Wonderful gets into some kind of scrape, always jump to his defense and immediately blame his nearby hoodlum friends. If this one seems to ring a not-too-distant bell, that's because it's partially recycled from our favorite verbal jousting responses (Chapter 4, slick item #10). Try this little script on for size: (I really love this one!)

"We all know Al isn't the problem here. He would never do something like this if he wasn't covering up for the rest of you simian thugs. If I find that you boys are taking advantage of my buddy, I'll dream up one of the worst consequences you've ever had! Al, just let me know if any of these wise guys give you trouble..."

5. Keep Little Secrets:
Try to build up a repertoire of "inside jokes" with Al. Ideally, these should be related to funny anecdotes that his buddies did not experience. Find out some interesting or humorous things about Al's personal life and make oblique eye-winking references to them in class.

6. Backhanded Compliments:
When your buddy Al does some academic task half right, use his worksheet as an example for the class. Tell his sorry friends that they need to follow Al's example and get with the program. From time to time make comments

about how you retold Al's last hysterical story or joke in the teacher's lounge and brought down the house. (You don't need to explain that there was just one other teacher in the lounge, and she may have been choking on that Garfield lasagna dish.)

Okay, put yourself in the place of Big Al's disciples. How long are you going to pay homage to this favored peer while he enjoys every privilege in the book, and you are still left out in the cold? Suppose your whole gang is in a prisoner of war camp (always a good word picture for school) and lucky Al keeps getting himself invited up to the commandant's private dining room for the evening meal. You are sitting there spooning cold swill, while Comrade Al is learning to use a lobster fork. Sooner or later, this strategy will pull the plug on the leader.

Strategy #2: Polarize The Gang Factions:

Here's one we blatantly lifted from a dozen or more *Mission Impossible* episodes. After the smoke cleared from his self-destructed tape recorder, Mr. Phelps would often find himself holding mug shots of rival bad guys from some obscure Balkan state. These guys represented internal factions of an evil political party that was considered an annoyance to the West. Mr. Phelps' secret assignment was to split up the power bloc, but do it without a show of force or any embarrassing head lines. You may remember the opening music score and pictures of each IM Force member being flashed on the screen? In recent OBM workshops I have used a brief video clip from the opening moments of the original *Mission Impossible* series to bring restless teachers back from the donuts and coffee table. If they got back in time, I'd reward that behavior by letting them see one of Mr. Phelps' tape recorder burn outs.

Classroom gang busting may seem like an impossible mission to many teachers. Suppose there is no real charismatic leader to go after (as in Strategy #1), but the group is still solid and non-compliant in your classroom. Not to worry here, either. Just like your work with Big Al, you will need to apply these innocuous strategies on a methodical, and daily basis. It's a very worthy OBM challenge....*should you decide to accept it.*

The basic plan with a very tight subgroup is to find internal differences which can be magnified and exploited. If the differences become stronger than the commonalties, the group will dissolve----and lose it's disruptive power in the classroom. As with other

OBM strategies, the teacher is not confrontive and seldom uses raw power. This is increasingly true the older the students are, and especially true when you have to look up to speak to them. Somewhere in this paragraph you'd probably expect me to add the "working smarter" phrase. But I won't, since you are already thinking about it. Below are a few polarization strategies. Perhaps you will think of many more:

1. Control Through Language:

Once you've sized up the group and found some representative factions, casually start to refer to multiple groups (never to one entity). *"Looks like the rappers are sharp today. They're gonna catch you basketball jocks if you don't stay focused on this assignment."* Notice how we split the gang simply by directing attention to some obvious differences?

Here's some more "group splitting" comments:

"All you athletes over there who had the Coach for Social Studies last year should be two steps ahead of these other boys."

"Why is it you north side guys always sit over there? Don't you trust these downtown guys? Do you have something against the way they slick their hair these days?"

"Seems like you three guys are the handsome musketeers of this crowd. So, what happened to these other fellows? A train wreck or something? How come they're not like you?"

"So, today we have the jocks over here and the cyber-techs right behind them...no wonder you guys have trouble communicating." Notice this gang was tentatively split through casual labeling, and then the teacher had the nerve to toss in the unfounded assumption that they can't communicate. More seed planting. Pretty soon this gang won't even be able to agree on who to beat up during lunch.

2. Control Through Competition:

In order to have competition, you have to have teams. No one should be too upset if the bad guys are divided up for some classroom competition. By the way, once you have created some teams, why not attach some colorful names to each of them. Later, make reference to individual ruffians as members (or alumni) of specific teams. Throughout the following days find reason to frequently use the team labels and draw various comparisons between the subgroups. Who knows, the labels might stick. *"Looks like the Buccaneers are leading the Raiders again today. These guys will need to slug it out in the last round of our Science Bowl..."*

(**Life Saving Hint**: Never set up a competition which pits the bad guys (as a united group) against the rest of the free world. You knew that, right?)

3. Control Through Friendly Wagers:

Sometimes a friendly wager might help to polarize factions of two groups. Suppose there are two strong personalities in a gang. It might be interesting to challenge the two to compete in a race, arm wrestling, or their knowledge of Hamlet. (One of these items may not fly.) Make some kind of silly bet and egg on the two sides. Let the champions of each faction strut around and boast a little like those brain dead professional wrestlers. Build up the importance of the competition and you might polarize the gang into two or more warring camps.

4. Control Through Suspicion:

Remember that stool pigeon in the *Stalog 17* movie? There was one rotten informant planted among the Allied prisoners, and everyone was kept on edge wondering who it was. The same can happen in school settings among difficult students. It's funny how nasty rumors can get started and virtually drag a gang operation to it's knees.

Remember OBM Principle # 4, the next best thing to compliance, is confusion. When a group of non-compliant students are caught up in the confusion of mistrust among themselves, they have little energy left for ruining the teacher's day. They might even settle down and learn something!

The teacher who is able to gather information in one location (even unfounded rumors and gossip at the *National Inquirer* level) and artfully "let them slip out" in another setting, can generate the illusion there is an "ear" within the gang. Spending some private time with several individual group members can help with the cross check of rumors, test the waters of trust within the group,....and generate cause for even more suspicion.

Another Compelling OBM War Story

I knew of one stealthy mid-school principal who came to the end of his rope with an in-house gang and decided to "go strategic" (i.e., rather than "ballistic"). Following a weekend vandalism incident he decided to round up the usual suspects for a mandatory interview that was to be hosted in his office. In preparation for the meeting, he sent all the suspects to an empty classroom where they were told to wait until they were called by the office secretary. As the story goes, this inept "Gum shoe" style principal had *forgotten* to turn off the intercom system in that vacant classroom. Bumbling and forgetful as he was, he had left the wall speaker in the silent "receive" mode. Wouldn't you know it, he had also mistakenly turned on an old tape recorder in his own office where the PA panel was located. You'd have sworn he had some kind of training with Matlock & Associates.

During the 15 to 20 minutes these local choir boys were waiting for their interview, this principal learned all kinds of things about the nature of crime on his own campus. He learned about old unsolved incidents, recent ones, and sinister agendas for the future. He heard angry statements like *"Hey Eddy, you and Rob really stepped in it this time. How could you be so stupid to spray paint your idiot slogan on the gym wall? That was even more stupid than Randy's flat tire job on all those busses. Now we're all taking heat....way to go Rufus!"* Of course Eddy responded with something like: *"Well at least I'm not going to take the big fall for you guys ripping off that raffle ticket money. Did you and LeRoy spend it all yet? I'll bet that's really why we're being called in right now."*

Our daring and resourceful principal was chuckling to himself during most of the dialog. He pictured himself as a good ol' boy Southern sheriff who had just bagged a speeding Winnebago full of intoxicated rock musicians. All was "business-as-usual" until he heard some talk like: *"We don't need to worry about that sorry principal, he's actually dumber than he looks. That loser will believe anything we tell him. You should have seen him eat up that last story about Lenny's History book being loaned to a crippled vet. He's such a jerk. All we need to do is stick together and use the same story...."* After some spirited pledges to secrecy and threats to any traitors, the boys soon learned from the secretary that they were to return to class "because the principal was too busy". The following day each boy was summoned to the office for his individual interview. Oddly enough, our "dumber than he looks" principal had watched his share of *Rockford Files*, *Magnum P.I.,* and *Remington Steele* re-runs. Without revealing identities or details, I can assure you that this entire gang was skillfully dismantled and brought to various levels of justice. The point to make here is that each gang member somehow (independently of the others) came to the conclusion he had been sold out by his comrades. What ever happened to trust?

Final Words:

When our difficult students band together, their oppositional traits tend to be magnified. However, gangs and other power blocs each have "built in" vulnerabilities that can be used to neutralize their threat to humanity. It's also especially helpful when they have interesting skeletons in the closet.

Chapter Eleven

Wacky Coupons and Behavior Permits
Taking Our Cue From Big Government Bureaucracy

It's a foundational tenet of big government. It's almost "the American Way". If people have a need, find a way to make a federal program out of it. At least write a three year grant to study the possibilities. Hey, even if a few folks start to show an interest in some new diversion, hobby, or mode of transportation---find a way to restrict it, license it, and tax it. Next, get the government presses rolling and turn out thousands of pages of confusing fine print regulations. Might also put a few more attorneys on payroll to help with interpretation.

Before we write off the cumbersome Big Government methods, let's stop and consider the hidden genius of bureaucratic regulation. We never claimed that OBM strategies were common sense. Rather, we tend to view them as "uncommon sense". In fact, the rational things are what people try *before* they consider our interventions. The present chapter suggests that one alternative way to control a behavior is to "regulate it to death". Why not target some silly nuisance behavior and strategically squeeze all the joy out of it---until our strong-willed student concludes that it's just not worth the effort.

OBM Example: Another Outrageous Way
To Neutralize The Gang Problem

Many of the disturbed high risk students we see on the school psychology case load are inordinately impressed with the gang subculture. These younger wannabees perceive our local gangs as viable family-substitutes. They see the rigors and danger of gang life to be miles ahead of the sad existence they now face. Somewhere inside they know it's all a dead end, but they are drawn like the proverbial moth to the proverbial flame. So far, nothing new.

In one of our infamous Friday afternoon supervision sessions, my state licensed *Far Side* staff was discussing the gang problem---and began to stray into some divergent OBM gang busting strategies. Here's a recently declassified summary of that meeting:

Suppose one of our toughest local mid schools was to concede defeat and publicly surrender to the gangs? (Not hardly, but stay with me.) Suppose the administration and staff all agreed to open the campus to gangs. In fact, any gang at all could be represented on campus *as long as it was done correctly*. Since we already have fairly accurate lists of each gang's membership, a special "by invitation only" assembly would be called to announce the details of opening the campus.

As a "modest" concession to being welcomed on campus, the punk fellowships would be asked to endorse the following policies: (I won't go into detail on all of them, but you can use your imagination....that's all we did.)

1. Each gang would have to complete a comprehensive application packet and compile a roster of active members on campus (sounds like a bowling league).

2. The school would collect a token registration fee, and take photographs for the new ID cards. Gang members could pose for group shots displaying their secret handsigns. These glossy photos would be available for purchase (to give to proud family members) and for later use in the annual gang yearbook).

3. Each gang would select a rehabilitated addict or ex-con as a sponsor (from a prepared list of community volunteers).

4. Each gang would be given a designated day when colors would be mandatory for all members. All those black tee-shirts and colors jackets would have to be clean and pressed on these days. If not, it would be the same as dis-ing the brothers. And that's not real healthy.

5. The school would recognize only two types of gangs: Easy Gangs and Tough Gangs. To get into an Easy Gang, all that would be required was a simple application form, the fee, and the ID card.

6. To gain admission to a Tough Gang (and who would join any other kind?), there would be a lengthy application and qualification process

involving rigorous training in physical fitness, self defense, problem solving, memorizing the code, secret handshake, the theme song; and creative expressions (e.g., barrio calligraphy, tattoos, emblems, decals, jewelry, etc.)

7. Weekly meetings would be required for each registered gang and the leader would have to file a brief written report with the Campus Gang Coordinator. A copy of the report would be retained by the Gang Secretary or some other designated member who is able to read. Special rooms and times would be scheduled and "security badges" (i.e., gang ID's with clips) displayed by all.

8. Each month would have a scheduled "combat day" in the gym fashioned after the showy "American Gladiator" competitions. Every gang would pay a small team entrance fee. All gangs would be expected to enter or lose face.

9. Any gang member having an attitude or behavior problem would be labeled a disgrace to his colors, and referred to the gang's own disciplinary committee (and I wouldn't even want to know what happens there!)

10. The academic curriculum would remain basically the same, except that names would be changed (e.g., Math would be "Money Issues"; PE would be "Street Games"; Social Studies would be "Neighborhood Sociology", Shop would be something like "Low Rider Research and Development", etc.).

11. Each month one gang would designate an ad hoc committee responsible for designing and placing fresh graffiti on selected walls and outdoor buildings. Individual gangs would have to raise money (legally, say through bake sales or tattoo-a-thons) to purchase their own paints and materials.

12. Each gang would submit one member's name to the gang coordinator for "Gangster of the Month" recognition. The winner's smiling face would then be published in the monthly newsletter: *The Rap Sheet*. This would be a great photo-op with a brief story covering the boy's gangster career, and maybe some cordial poses with his proud mother and her smiling boyfriend. The central picture would show the winner in his gang colors receiving a plaque from the glad-all-over school principal.

We could go on and on with ways to institutionalize and regulate gangs, and eventually "squeeze the joy" out of counter culture rebellion. Once the local gangs conceded to "a few rules" to the establishment (Believe it or not flower child, that's us these days) they would be marked for neutralization. Can you imagine youth gangs turning into Boy Scout troops and sports teams? Can you imagine kids *dropping out* of gangs---as an act of youthful rebellion? What about keeping those grades up to remain gang eligible? Think of those slick varsity jackets and maybe some regional scholarships to attend inner city gang workshops? Enough already. Let's get back to the more focused topic of OBM coupons and permits.

Using "The Paper Chase" to Control Behavior:

I think we have made a case for the age old concept: *If you can't beat 'em,...regulate 'em.* Turning away from the gang issues, suppose little first grade Robert is obsessed with tattle tales. Everyday he makes a dozen spy reports on peers who are "playing too rough", "not sharing the ball", and "talking mean". It seems Robert is intent on controlling the class by using poor Ms. Farnsworth as his enforcer. Since this fellow is intent on knowing and using "the rules", he is also a candidate for OBM behavior permits.

Our Ms. Farnsworth, a portly mild mannered elementary teacher, ---is also secretly an accomplished OBM practitioner! She is particularly effective in certain OBM methods, simply because no one would ever suspect her deeper strategic motives. She has already attempted to redirect, understand, counsel, and reward Robert toward more pro-social living. All to no avail. Turning to OBM methods, this teacher will now stop trying to extinguish the tattle tale compulsion, and begin to license, tax, and regulate it. She has prepared a supply of bright colored "Tattle Tale Coupons" with a catchy graphic and fine print instructions. On the next page is a partial script of her private visit with little Robert:

Wacky Coupon Script

"Hello there Robert. I just wanted to thank you for caring about the behavior of all the students in our class. However, in order to save time, you need to start keeping your mind on only the most important behavior problems. Also, because my time is very limited these days, I'm going to need to charge something for helping you control student behavior. (Note: The teacher maintains a straight face as only that crafty Ms. Farnsworth can do.) *I have a supply of coupons here that are each good for reporting on one student. If you needed to tell me about two boys who were fighting, of course you would need to give me how many coupons?* (The bewildered child answers) *That's right, and you would also need to save your coupons for reporting only the most important problems.*

It would be too bad if you used up all your coupons right away and then you saw someone cutting in line. You wouldn't have any Tattle Tale Coupons left to use, and so I couldn't listen to that important report. You can only get coupons in the morning before class. And you can only buy five each day. The way you pay for your supply of coupons is by telling me one good student behavior you saw recently in class. That's it. You'll get your five coupons and be off on a new day of behavior watching."

You get the idea. Ms. Farnsworth can reduce the number of daily coupons in the future. She might also offer some incentive for "saving up" coupons (e.g., spending them on some pro-social activity). One hidden benefit of coupon therapy is that the student becomes very sensitized to how often he performs the target behavior. Who knows, he might even start to budget his "reporting" episodes. Another fringe benefit is that the particular nuisance behavior has now been given a name, and is out on the table for some frank teacher-student dialog during the day.

What About Bob?

You may recall an outrageous movie plot where the self-absorbed Dr. Leo Marvin used the rigors of *Death Therapy* to rid Bob of his multiple phobias. In the same manner, think of all those gross, goofy, or dependent classroom behaviors that might be reduced by requiring coupons? And guess who controls the coupons? To follow our earlier Big Government illustration, that's like asking who controls the Federal Reserve printing presses. Below is a sampling of the Wacky Coupons we have deftly used with oppositional students.

1. **Out-Of-Seat For No Good Reason Coupon:** This is one to collect from the habitual classroom wanderer. Isn't it high time he started paying for those little excursions to the pencil sharpener? The coupon is good for only 60 seconds and mine always carry an expiration date.

2. **Voluntary Time-Out:**
Here's one I've seen used for multiple purposes. You can give (or sell) one to the classroom hot head, and instruct him to use it *before* he gets in trouble. It might even help this student learn to monitor his anger level. The teacher might suggest the slogan: "Use it, before you lose it". Get it? Another use is for the semiconscious student who spends most of the afternoon pushing ZZZZ's with his head down. Enforce the no sleeping in class rule, and require that he pay one coupon for 10 minutes of "resting" in the Time Out booth. If he needs more rest, he'll have to get sharp and purchase more coupons (or stop watching *MTV* until 3AM).

3. **Getting-The-Last-Word Coupon**:
 This one is perfect for the highly verbal but oppositional student. It may be redeemed for permission to have the last word while making the usual excuses or insisting he is right. Imagine the teacher's joy as she ends a

minor disciplinary consult with the student by (automatically, with a knowing smile) stretching out her hand for a coupon. This really gets to these kids. Their last word self-justifications are deeply reflexive. I recall one kid so upset with himself for falling into a "last word" coupon charge that he folded his arms across his chest and gritted his teeth for five minutes. The teacher's facial expressions said it all---at last she had some control.

4. **Bugging Coupon:**

Here's a multipurpose permit which pokes some humor at students who do things to annoy their peers. Whenever the problem child is caught in some harassment of a classmate, he is required to atone for his sins by giving the coupon to his victim. Later, the victim student can redeem the coupon for cash, jewelry, vacation trips, or major appliances. (not).

5. **Bad Attitude Coupon:**

Do you have a student who gets in a foul pouty mood and seems bent on maintaining it for the whole day? For these "attitudinally challenged" students, why not require the payment of a coupon? Our old stand by has this fine print: *"Present this coupon to your teacher for the right to enjoy 10 minutes of really bad attitude during class time."* Students who are in the process of enjoying their negative 'tude time have been required to display the coupon somewhere conspicuously on their desk. I've seen some cases where the coupon was worn over a shirt button as a badge. At the end of the 10 minute period the teacher can announce that it's time to go back to "normal mood" (and some kids will say "Oh? Okay..." and change instantly). If the bad mood isn't ready to blow over just yet, simply ask for a second coupon.

6. **Whining, Grumbling & Complaining Coupon:**

This one is for a more vocal case of bad attitude. Why let that malcontent sit there spitting and sputtering for free? Charge him for it and at least you maintain some semblance of leadership. Our coupon carries the instructions: *"Present this coupon for the privilege of being miserable in class for 5 minutes."* Some kids will need to earn a good supply of these, since the 5 minute time slots go by pretty fast.

7. **Goofiness Coupon:**

We have two different styles of coupon for this theme. One shows a silly monkey who's been off his ritalin for days. The other is my favorite for more sophisticated adults with a classic Groucho character. On both, the instructions state: *"This coupon may be redeemed for permission to act goofy, silly, or disgusting for a period of five (5) minutes."*

Originally I designed the monkey coupon for an elementary teacher who had received one of my difficult Special Education students into her afternoon class. This kid delighted in outlandish classroom interruptions which drove the teacher bananas and tended to alienate the other students. The teacher loved the coupon idea and enhanced it to the max. Whenever Rowdy Raymond looked like he was ready to launch into one of his show-stoppers, the teacher would quickly collect one Goofiness Coupon and then give him the center spotlight. Her announcement would be something like: *"Class, can we have everyone's attention over here. Please stop whatever you're doing for just a moment. Raymond is ready to entertain us with one of his memorable comic routines. Ray, you're on!"* At that point rowdy Raymond would just stand there with a sheepish expression. The teacher wouldn't let him sit down for a while since the floor time had cost him a valuable coupon. Believe it or not, this OBM teacher extinguished the class interruptions in about two or three trials. (Go ahead, compare that with smiley stickers.)

We have generated dozens of these things, but you get the picture. When you run into a chronic behavior that has resisted the usual attempts at extinction, you might consider using Wacky Coupons and unusual behavior permits. If you can't stop the behavior: license it, tax it, and regulate it to death. At last we have learned something valuable from big government bureaucracy!

For your convenience, we are including a bunch of sample coupons and permits on the following pages. Go ahead and use them right-out-of-the-box, or develop your own custom red tape for the joys of the regulatory paper chase.

Voluntary Time-Out

COUPON

Present this coupon and receive ten (10) minutes of quiet time at the *Time Out* place.

Coupon Expires on: _____

Out-Of-Seat
for no good reason

COUPON

Present this coupon for permission to be out of your seat and do some unnecessary task for one (1) minute.

BUGGING
Coupon

This coupon may be redeemed for permission to BUG others and make a general nusiance of yourself for 5 minutes

<u>Special Rules:</u> You may not use your normal voice while bugging.   Left eye must remain closed.   No criminal behaviors.

GETTING–THE–LAST–WORD
Coupon

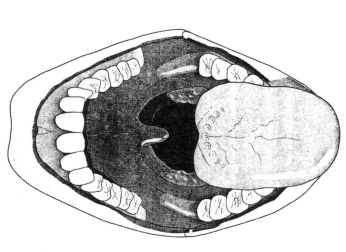

This coupon may be redeemed for permission to have the last word while making the usual excuses or insisting you are right.

(Good for a one minute defense)

GOOFINESS
Coupon

This coupon may be redeemed for permission to act goofy, silly, or disgusting for a period of five (5) minutes

Special Rules: This coupon void if no one smiles within one minute of seeing your goofiness.

GOOFINESS
Coupon

This coupon may be redeemed for permission to act goofy, silly, or disgusting for a period of five (5) minutes

Special Rules: This coupon void if no one smiles within one minute of seeing your goofiness.

Whining Grumbling & Complaining

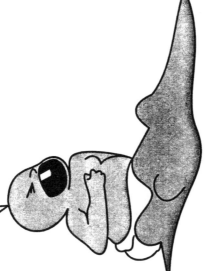

COUPON

Present this coupon for the privilege of being miserable in class for 5 minutes.

Coupon Expires on: _____

Bad Attitude

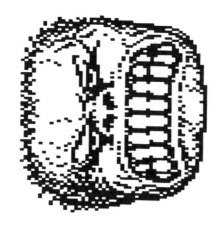

COUPON

Present this coupon for the right to enjoy 10 minutes of really bad attitude during class time.

Coupon Expires on: _____

PANIC CARD!

When Life gets tense, use this card for urgent care at the school counselor's office

(Not good for getting out of trouble!)

Tattle Tale
COUPON

Present this coupon for the right to report on the evil misbehavior of one other student.

Coupon Expires on: _____

BUSTED!

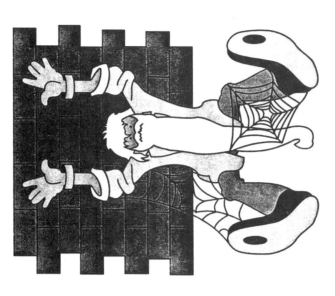

Looks like you need some
TIME OUT to cool down

State of
CONFUSION
Coupon

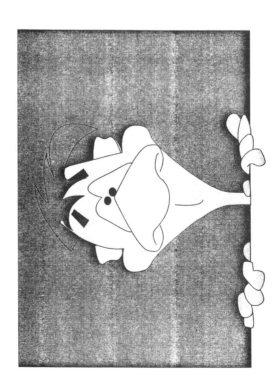

Feeling totally confused today?
Present this coupon for some extra help
in understanding that impossible classwork.

Chapter Twelve

Those Voices In Your Head

Borrowing Some Needed Clout

Sometimes the classroom teacher has little in the way of direct raw power over the strong-willed student. Dah...what's new? However, through skillful observation of the difficult student, it may become apparent that there is someone else who *does* hold considerable influence. That someone may have real clout that is rooted beyond your classroom setting. It's always a thing of beauty to see smart aleck Bernard (smack in the middle of his resistance routine) suddenly mellow out like someone flipped a switch. Here's your hard core oppositional student going through his usual act, when suddenly he glimpses Major Player #1 strolling into the classroom. An instant conversion experience takes place before your eyes. You turn to smile at this awesome influence who has entered the class. (Note: This is also the time when I like to lean over to impossible Bernard and whisper: "Keep it up. That looks so real! Maybe we can convince him (or her) you're doing just fine....").

Most frequently this Major Player is a tough parent who is frustrated at the reports coming home from the principal's office. By the way, you can also bet your next-year's raise that the other parent on the team--mother or father-- is much more permissive, and maintains some kind of enabling or protective alliance with little Bernard. That's just the way it is. Sometimes that powerful, influential person is a favorite teacher, a sports coach, or a doting grandparent. Other times our Major Player is the Chinese immigrant custodian who teaches martial arts, a charismatic bus driver, a "Joe Friday" probation officer, or maybe it's mysterious Uncle Carmine who always carries that violin case. Whoever it is---he or she *has got the clout.*

Of course, we can't help but wonder during these brief transformations: "How could we bottle this magical influence and use it later?" ...So glad you asked. As it is, our top notch team of OBM researchers have labored far into the night, toiling over this very question. After years of study and painstaking field tests, we have developed a simple method of preserving emotional influence for later classroom use!

Canned Voices

If little Atila H. won't listen to you, why not put a convincing voice in his head? In the noble spirit of cooperation, we have often invited our influential "Major Player" to a private meeting where one or more special messages are recorded on cassette. These are then labeled: "Last Ditch Warning" or "Encouragement", and filed away for strategic OBM use. Later, when that power monger is up to his old tricks again, he soon finds himself slumped in the Time Out corner with headphones in place. He is then overwhelmed by a familiar authoritative voice in his head reminding him of what he really wants to be doing.

After years of real-world use, and dozens of hilarious war stories, we still aren't sure which recording methods work best. Here's a few of the procedures that have been used:

1. Spontaneous Jive:

Some parents and "significant other adults" are comfortable and secure with taking a microphone in hand and telling it like it is. They often have a special patter that has been developed over many years of relating to the child. If the OBM teacher simply tells them that a few words are needed on respect, back talk, and getting to work on time, these folks are off and running with the finest pedantic rhetoric you ever heard.

For example, try to picture how this one works in the Black culture. Young Willie has all the potential in the world. He could be a doctor, lawyer, or even a mid-school teacher. But he's also afflicted with strong oppositional traits. His dear old Cosby-like dad picks up the microphone for a five minute "visit" that comes off smooth and authoritative. This parent has plans for Willie and isn't about to let him smart mouth his way out of 5th grade. Okay, and how about a well-informed Aunt Phoebe who is also invested in Willie's education. You can't possibly measure her verbal skills with any known technology.   She immediately captures the microphone and gives poor Willie a dose of what-for that builds up like a steam locomotive, rumbles on through the country, and goes the distance like a Southern preacher. You've gotta love this stuff!

A good part of my school psychology practice has been based in the rural communities of the culturally diverse Southwestern desert. I recall working there with a squirmy resistant Navajo boy who was a perfect 3rd grade candidate for some OBM "cooling of his jets". A planning meeting was set up and a large contingent of extended family members arrived at the school. Similar to some other ethnic groups, the Navajo people have some definite leanings toward matriarchal leadership---especially in such matters as child discipline and choosing which rodeo events their husband will enter. Sure enough, when the family group was seated, it soon became obvious that the mother and aunts were not the ultimate source of authority. Difficult questions were discussed briefly in English and then carefully translated into Navajo for the boy's grandmother who was sitting quietly and majestically at the rear of my office. All heads turned in unison to receive her wisdom and final decisions on the boy's fate. I would then wait for the English interpretation to come back my way and then proceed with the matters at hand.

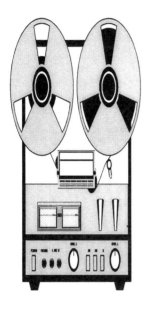

Okay let's see how many rocket scientists we have reading our Handbook. When it came time to ask that someone make a taped "warning" or "re-direction" message for this boy, who do you suppose I asked? Very good! This OBM stuff must be creating geniuses among us. I respectfully explained that we could really use a brief message from grandma to help this kid get his mind back on his work, and on the need for respect toward his frazzled teacher. To this day, I do not know what grandma said on the tape. No doubt, I had run in to another high verbal skills speaker. This grandma stayed behind in my office and spoke sincerely and confidently into the microphone. The teacher was later provided with this classic tape and asked to keep it in a safe place (e.g., near the Civil Defense supplies). Each time there was some problem with defiance, the boy was sent to a bean bag chair and required to listen to his tape. Grandma's message seemed to work some kind of magic on this kid ---and all went well until the tape got lost!

I understand that the kid loved his special tape and somehow convinced his rookie teacher to allow him to take it home overnight. Oddly enough, the tape disappeared at home. We could never relocate grandma who lived a hundred miles out on the Reservation,....and everyone concluded that the teacher needed more smart pills. Her penance was to suffer through the remainder of that millennia-long semester without grandma's help.

2. Talk-Show Interviews:

Suppose the parent or last-year's-coach is willing to help out, but not quite sure how to handle a hot microphone. In this situation, I just invite him/her/them for a private interview "about" the child. We put the tape recorder out on the table and simply chat for awhile. I will often throw out some lead questions and let my guests address the child by name. Some of the classic pump-primers include:

"So,...what are the serious concerns that bring you all the way in to school today?"

"I understand you got some ugly news from school that has made you pretty upset?"

"Do you have something important that you need to say to Rocky?"

"I can tell by your clinched fists and gritted teeth that you have something on your mind."

During these interviews we are always mindful that the noncompliant student will some day be listening to our tape as an "overheard" conversation between adults. As long as the parent is doing well, I let him or her carry the ball throughout the interview. Somewhere along the way, I will naively ask if the parent *really* expects the child to accept these comments and suggestions. The intent is to have my interview guest make some clear assertions. I really want the parent to sense that his/her credibility is on the line. Check out some of these classic exemplars:

> "Justin, listen son...when you hear my voice telling you to chill out and go back to work, it's like I'm right there in the class talking to you. I expect you will do exactly as I'm asking......."

> "Billy, if you are allowed to hear this message, consider it your last chance to avoid big trouble at home. Here's what I want you to do as soon as you finish the tape......."

> "Now that you have listened to my little message, I'm giving you one chance to follow my instructions, like right away....or else go back to class and keep up your old routine. It's your choice, and you know I'll be told whether you respected my tape....."

Sometimes the parent speakers will branch off into what grandma would think, how deceased uncle Joe would be so proud, or the fact that the family reputation is at stake. Coaches remind the kid of school pride, eligibility for playing in the next game, and how the guys on the team are counting on him to try hard. Juvenile probation officers are a different breed of cat. They remind the willful student of his contract with the court that calls for full compliance with school conduct rules. These guys evoke memories of courtrooms, stern judges, and uniformed officers. For some local tough guys, that "empathetic" JPO voice on the tape sounds like "Eastwood with an attitude" and brings up vivid images of a gray weekend cell at the detention facility. Hey, I'll take whatever clout I can distill on the tape.

3. Idiot Cards and Prepared Scripts:

This one reminds me of an old TV commercial for cars which attempted to poke fun at the phony testimonials concocted by some (other) Detroit competitors. We are presented with a gaunt middle aged man in a disgusting plaid leisure suit. He is trembling and sweating like a goosey Don Knotts, awkwardly posed with one arm along the roof of his car. This middle-aged picture of sincerity swallows hard and musters a cracked voice to announce: "In my own words.....This... is truly...a fine...automobile (forced smile)."

Actually, this is about as credible as some tapes I have received from clueless parents who are allowed to hide behind a prepared script. It's might be better than nothing, but a script always cries out for enhancement. Below are some introductory comments for the parent (or other speaker) and then a sample "canned" statement. It might best be used as an example of some content issues, before working on the *real message*. We will assume the "guest speaker "is a concerned parent and that the malefactor student is his/her erring wayward son.

Here's a good opener statement to warm up our respected speaker: *"You have been asked to record a message to this student because of your influence in his life and his obvious respect for your guidance. Imagine that your son is on the verge of "getting in trouble" at school. Suppose he is worked up about something and is hurling caution to the wind. Suppose he is about ready to throw a fit in class or become grossly disrespectful to a teacher. What could you say at this point to redirect your child. What words could you use to transmit your parental authority at home to a classroom situation?"* Often, this is enough to prime the pump and get the parent speaker flowing with all manner of statements and platitudes.

On the following page is a sample script,... just in case you need a jump start today.

Sample Script For
Parent Message

Note: Be sure to select a good background musical score to create the right mood. Our favorites include: Greensleaves, The William Tell Overture, or the theme to Hawaii Five-0.

"Joseph, this is your dad speaking and I want you to listen very carefully to what I have to say. I want you to listen just like I was standing right there talking to you. Whatever respect you would give me in person, is the same respect I want you to give to my voice message right now.

If you are listening to this tape, it means that you are probably about to get into some kind of trouble....but you haven't actually done that yet. Maybe you've said something or done something that has your teacher concerned. We all understand that school problems are normal for everybody.....the work you have to do, the things other kids do, the rules the teachers have to enforce...all that can get anyone upset from time to time....BUT, none of that stuff justifies acting up or disrespecting your teachers. Nothing that has happened so far today gives you the right to throw a fit or say anything disrespectful. Kids who do that kind of stuff are announcing to the world that they can't manage their own program, and that they need outside controls.

No matter how right you are, or how good your ideas are....nothing allows you to act up today. This message is your opportunity to take a few minutes to calm down, think straight, and get yourself under control again. Maybe you should just take a few deep breaths and try to think of the end of school today....Imagine yourself leaving school and coming home with no black cloud over your head...no negative messages coming home to me. All I'll know is that you used the tape successfully and I'll be proud of you.

Of course we all know that some kids who aren't in control need some kind of penalty or consequence at home to help steer them away from misbehavior. It could be what you need today. I'm not sure. Only you can decide to respect my message, and after you finish this tape your behavior will tell me your true decision.

I know you are a smart kid. I believe you can make good decisions...even when they are really hard decisions. That's cause you're my kid, and I'm betting everything I've got on you being a winner today. I'll be waiting to learn of your good decision about respectful school behavior."

Try a "RAT" Card for Feedback

Notice how the parent speaker (above) seems to be expecting some kind of feedback about how the tape affected his son's behavior? Whenever a parent comes in for a planning session (and his/her private "recording session") we also take time to decide on some kind of system for immediate feedback. It's only right that the speaker receive information on how well his eloquent message controlled his offspring. We feel that these "calm down" messages tend to put the parent on the spot. Everyone is waiting to see if he or she really does have any clout. You will recall that we like to select only those speakers who already seem to have some transmittable influence.

Anyway, why not use a simple prepared card to "rat" on the student? We have cleverly padded the meaning of our "RAT" card with the acronym: *Re-telling Actions Taken*. This card is a report of his behavioral decision following any encounters with that persuasive voice in his head. The RAT card also bears the student and teacher signatures. Call us old fashioned, but we like to use a carbon paper sandwich with two or three identical RAT cards. Of course, it's not that we don't trust our non-compliant student to deliver the original card home to daddy. No, no, no...It's just our quirky way of keeping track of the program. Besides, we keep hearing of alien abductions and drive-by note grabbing when messages are sent home like that. Here's the deal.

We send the bottom copy home *that afternoon* with the student. The original (top) RAT card is kept for a near future parent-teacher meeting; and if there is a middle copy, it could show up any day in the future mail, or at the parent's place of business (depending on the current level of trust in the home). It's all arranged at the first meeting, and you'd be surprised at the honesty and mutual trust that's generated. Take a look at the sample RAT card we've tucked in at the end of the chapter.

Other Nagging Details and Considerations

1. Encourage your speaker to use the jargon and native language used in the home.

2. Why not produce two or three brief tapes and rotate their use?

3. Use the taped messages as a quasi-Time Out consequence. Provide a quiet place and headphones for private listening.

4. For a mobile consequence, provide a Walkman tape player and have the student walk around the track or playground while listening.

5. Have the student produce his own self-control tape, or (better yet) write out a partial script for his parent to use!

6. For parents of defiant students (who are still communicating), suggest that they tape a private dialog "about" the student which ends in direct behavioral instructions. Just a thought.

7. Why not tape a "secret" group discussion about the student---with several key family members---and end with everyone agreeing on some direct behavioral instructions?

RAT CARD

THIS FEEDBACK CARD CONFIRMS THAT

_____

STUDENT'S NAME

LISTENED TO A TAPED MESSAGE AT

TIME: _____   DATE: _____

TRIGGER SITUATION:

_____

RESPONSE TO THE TAPED MESSAGE:

☞   _IMPROVEMENT   DETERIORATION_   ☞

+3 +2 +1 0 -1 -2 -3

CANDID COMMENTS:

TEACHER: _____

Chapter Thirteen

Outrageous B-Mod
Some Parting Shots

Salute To The Pioneers:

This handbook has introduced only a sample of the OBM strategies already developed. We need to keep in mind, however, that nearly every form of classroom behavior management owes some recognition to the early learning theorists such as J.B. Watson, E.R. Guthrie, E.L. Thorndike, E.C. Tolman, and even the late great B.F. Skinner, himself. As you might guess, these deeply cerebral theory builders would turn over in their graves if they could see some of the stuff in the past chapters. Our grinning apologies to the ivory tower. It might be said that OBM methods represent the basic principles of human learning---*with an attitude.*

My own academic history includes some fortunate encounters with many contemporary psychologists who are making a difference in their choosen areas of study. I learned of the above classic theorists from my first graduate advisor, Dr. Steve Davis, a front line learning theorist himself, and unabashed rat runner. He's currently at Emporia State Univerisity, Kansas, in case you want to send your kids to a solid undergraduate program, where there's more studying than frisbee throwing. When it comes to learning principle *applications* in the classroom (i. e., hard-core applied behavior analysis), I have learned more from Dr. Jim Koller than any other single source. Professor Koller is active in lecturing, consulting, and training doctoral-level school psychologists at the University of Missouri-Columbia. I have mentioned these two mentors in the OBM Handbook, with the hope that there will be no attempt to recind my graduate degrees.

Actually, there are a few other writers---primarily psychotherapists----who should also bare some of the blame for the emergence of OBM classroom methods. Foremost among these is Milton Erikson, a maverick psychiatrist-hypnotist who probably never dangled a pocket watch or suggested that anyone's eyes were growing heavy. I'll bet he was also clueless regarding academic learning theory. In his own unorthodox way, Erikson told delightful metaphoric stories that invited his patients to slip into productive daydream trances. During a period when most "therapy" was bound up in lengthy analysis, Erikson also master minded hundreds of elegant homework assignments that disrupted "symptoms" and freed up his patients to make wise choices.

Beyond Eriksonian hypnosis there's a bus load of contemporary practitioners who write, lecture, and do training demonstrations---primarily for social workers and family therapists. These folks all do similar work but describe their own particular brands of therapy with such labels as: "Brief", "Solution Focused", "Systems" and "Strategic". In case you are driven to read more in this fascinating field, some of the heavy weight names include: Jay Haley, Cloe' Madanes, Bill O'Hanlon, and one of my favorite iconoclasts, Joel Bergman. There's also a pair of irreverent therapists who go by the names Bandler & Grinder. These guys have worked for years trying to systematize a raft of really slick hypnotherapy tricks. When you consider that their first book bore the title: *Frogs Into Princes,* you'll probably understand why their "outrageous" work is welcome here. They even came up with a credible sounding name for their craft: Neuro Linguistic Programming (NLP).

If you've made it thus far through the handbook, you now have some glimpses of what goes on in our live OBM workshops. While these captive trainees do receive an extensive notebook of our "classic" OBM materials, the core strategies remain basically the same as those before you. On the other hand, it might be mentioned that my counseling staff has now cataloged over 51 separate OBM interventions. That's too many chapters, even if you did take your ritalin. Besides, many of these off beat classroom strategies have not yet been tamed for civilian use! We'll be seeing you again in the future.

Some Words on Ethical Practice:

Because at times we may seem a bit over zealous with this OBM stuff, here's the part where we try to put the outrageous methods in some perspective. First, as therapists, consultants, and evaluators, we do a full spectrum of clinical work. During an average day in the schools or at my clinical office, I do many other interventions beside OBM. The whole idea of developing these techniques was to broaden the range of methods available to the classroom teacher (certainly not to limit them!). Teachers with multiple skills are more confident than "single tool" educators. Use what works. Get rid of what doesn't. And we'd be down right proud if you'd just keep our OBM strategies in mind as an option.

Some readers (not you of course) may also need to be reminded that OBM methods are intended for intense interpersonal situations where the teacher must deal personally with an obstinate student. These fancy ploys and gimmicks are not meant to replace good planning, district-wide policies, and a general class management program. They're also not intended for ordinary even-tempered students who are just having a bad day. Save OBM for the kids who are really wired to resist.

Also for the record, we never use or recommend OBM techniques on abused, or seriously emotionally disturbed students. We take care of our hurting kids in other supportive ways. Besides, that still leaves a few genuine hard core students filing into your next hour's class. These are the kids who we believe can profit from some fast-acting and witty stratagems.

Famous Last Words:

A good universal maxim to use in selecting a particular OBM method would be the Golden Rule from the Master Instructor. You've probably heard of His "do unto others" principle. Here's our reframed application: Suppose you were an impossible student who was bent on ruining your school career. (I know this is hard to imagine, but bear with me.) If one of your teachers knew of a painless but effective way to redirect your self-defeating energy, would you fault that teacher for applying an OBM intervention? If your answer is "No problem, go for it!", and if you really do care about effectively guiding your students, then welcome to the fascinating world of strategic management.

Appendix I
YOUR O-B-M POTENTIAL

How well does your personality and life experience match the classic OBM model?
Answer these cryptic inquires "honestly" and score yourself below.

1. When you arrived home from school, did your mother often find "Kick Me" stickers attached to your sweater?

   ___Not   ___Yes, but elementary ___Yes, through
             grades only   college

2. When you used to read the **Calvin & Hobbs** comic strip, were you:

   ___Entertained by ___Flooded with ideas ___Prompted to
     his struggles   for tougher   lecture this kid
     with authority   discipline   on obedience

3. When you are approached by "hustlers" on the street, do you frequently:

   ___Hit *them* up for ___Ask if they accept ___Let them select any
     spare change   Visa/MC   bill from your wallet

4. When you first saw **The Sting** (with Redford & Newman) were you:

   ___Captivated by ___Mildly amused ___Asking if you
     the plot   missed something

5. When you watch **Columbo** interview a crook, do you think:

   ___"Genius at work" ___This guy should have ___Are there any sit-coms
             retired in 1978   on the other
                         channels?

6. When you see **Far Side** calendar pages, do you:

   ___Xerox the gems ___Smile and move on ___Seek help with
     for future   interpretations
     chuckles

7. Do you find syndicated detective shows like **The Rockford Files, Simon & Simon, Remington Steele,** and **Magnum, PI** to be:

   ___Intriguing plots ___Good for a few laughs ___Disgusting escapism
     and "set ups"

8. Do you feel lost and frustrated in taking this self-assessment?

   ___No, and I just ___I see where it's going ___Yes, it's moronic
     thought of   and degrading
     some more items!

9. Over the years, have you frequently heard the comment: **"You just don't get it".**

   ___Not   ___Only from supervisors ___Frequently, and it still
                         makes no sense to me

SCORING: Give yourself about 100 points for each response on the left, about 5 points for each response in the center position, and probably zero points for all others.

Your OBM Total

INTERPRETATION:

    700 and above: Definite OBM career potential! (Get liability insurance)
    30 to 699: With guidance and flexible thinking, you'll enjoy OBM
    zero to 29: Please review the handbook "Disclaimer"

Before you "get tough"....

Some Questions To Ask About
PROBLEM BEHAVIOR

_____1. How chronic (i.e., long lasting or habitual) and severe is it? Could I live with it if I slightly reduced my expectations? How different is this particular behavior from the class mean?

_____2. Does this particular behavior defy my authority as the classroom teacher? Does it impede my opportunity to teach?....or the learning opportunity of other students?

_____3. Have I stated in clear specific terms just which behaviors are required in my classroom? Have I communicated exactly what I want from this student?

_____4. Have I discovered what it is that really bugs me about this student's behavior? Just what is my emotional reaction to this student as a person? Does he or she "remind" me of someone? Is there an unspoken clash between our temperament styles?

_____5. Am I struggling with stressors in my personal life which reduce my ability to tolerate certain misbehaviors? Am I taking care of myself; and do I feel good about my profession?

_____6. All behavior is caused by something. Have I determined what motivates this student's problem behavior? Here are just a few possibilities to consider:
> a. A blatant quest for power or control?
> b. An excessive need for attention?
> c. A displacement of anger toward a parent?
> d. "Modeling" of a sick behavior from home?
> e. A manipulation strategy spawned out of
>   street survival needs?
> f. A hidden revenge motive?

_____7. Is this student's misbehavior a result of repeated failure and frustration with the standard curriculum? If so, have I reasonably tried to adapt or modify the curriculum?

_____8. Have I determined if this problem behavior is **"pre-meditated"**, a **"reflexive habit",** or an issue of **"developmental immaturity"**? My intervention planning will vary accordingly.

Behavioral interventions are not "one size fits all". Keep each of these items in mind as you work through the OBM Handbook.

Barry T. Christian, Ph.D. (1997)

OBM Guide To
Subtle Transformations

You're getting sleepy, sleepy, sleepy...

Throughout the OBM Handbook we have illustrated dozens of unorthodox techniques for taking control of disruptive and oppositional behavior. You may notice that many of our elaborate OBM strategies include one or more of the "Subtle Transformations" in this list. In most of our strategies, it is essential that our daring and resourceful OBM teacher request some early minor variations in the problem behavior. After explaining how the oppositional student is to continue pretending, practicing, or performing that disgusting jerk-like behavior, the savvy OBM teacher will also add something like:

"....Oh, and by the way, could I ask that you do your pretend behavior just a bit differently..."

As insignificant as it may seem, requiring even the slightest alteration in the "raw" misbehavior will put the teacher on the road to blissful control. Some old familiar terms like "shaping" and "successive approximation" may also come to mind right now. Below are some of the basic types of change that the OBM teacher might request from the classroom tyrant as he is "doing" his routine.

1. Change the *frequency* of that annoying behavior.

Examples:

"That pencil tapping habit is still only fairly disruptive. I mean probably most kids in the class are bothered by it....but not all. If I'm going to learn how to handle really disruptive behaviors, you're going to have to tap a lot more each class period....maybe twice as much...even when you don't feel like it."

"What you're doing is okay so far as it goes, but for effective development of a whiny sounding voice, we're going to need at least ten more practice trials each morning."

"Sometimes you resist things and argue with me ---just as we planned, but other times I see you just going along with the rest of the class and doing really good work. If our little program is going to work, I'm going to need to see a lot more strong-looking resistance behaviors each day...."

2. Change the **rate** of those vexing habits.

Examples:

"When you're doing one of those practice tantrums, try kicking your feet a lot faster, like you really mean it..."

"Whenever you are doing your excuse-making in Math class, could you hit me with at least three crazy reasons your work isn't done. You know, like bang, bang, bang! **Three off-the-wall reasons real quick...**"

"I need to have you come up to my desk at least three times each class period and urgently request to see the nurse."

3. Change the **duration** of that obnoxious routine.

Examples:

"I thought you had your getting-the-last-word performance down pretty well until yesterday. It seems you're slipping a little. Remember the deal. You're supposed to keep up the arguing and whining **during the entire time** *I'm passing out the worksheets. Somehow, your complaining over the last couple days hasn't lasted long enough for me to really practice my management skills."*

"That angry voice sounds pretty sincere, but you need to **hold the mean looking face just a bit longer.** *Try holding it until at least two other students seem to notice you're upset..."*

4. Change the **time of day** that the heinous act is committed in class.

Examples:

"In order to have you give it your best shot, let's have you start the foot tapping and wiggling-in-your-seat practice trials **a lot earlier in class.**"

*"Your grumbling noises have sounded very real during 3rd hour Science. And they have been very helpful to me. However, I need to ask for another favor. Would you be able to **shift your grumbling noises to 2nd hour** Social Studies ....and make them sound just as real there?"*

"Instead of waiting till afternoon *for your sleepy spells, I need you to pretend to go to sleep at the end of 2nd hour.*

5. Change the **physical location** where this loathsome charade is performed.

*"Could you **just move over to this desk** here when it's time to do your special practice behaviors?"*

*"This pouting skill is important enough that I need to have you pick a better area...say, **in the back of the class**...to practice without interruption."*

*"Could we change your pretend behaviors just a little for today? I'd like you to keep raising your hand and asking me impossible questions, but this time **only if your desk is turned a little side-ways**...so you look more confused."*

6. Change the student's **physical posture** while acting out the vile sequence.

Examples:

*"Next time you do your pretend arguing behaviors for me, could you **stick your chin out** (like this) just to remind me to stay sharp?"*

*"Let's have a secret signal. Whenever you are doing your I-hate-this-class routine, could you remember to **keep one hand clenched in a tight fist**? That will let me know you're trying to do your best job right at that time...."*

*"How 'bout **leaning forward in your desk just a little** whenever you're pretending to have one of those head aches? That will be my signal to ask if you're feeling sick..."*

7. Change the **intensity** of that contemptible conduct.

> Examples:
>
> *"Could you remember to resist my instructions **more strongly and openly** toward the beginning of Math class?...and then you are welcome to just relax and participate normally (or) surprise me and practice some more resisting later on."*
>
> *"Let's try this...in Art or Literature class, (you choose one) I'd like you to pretend to be **even more slow...very, very slow**....in starting your work. Look around and make sure you're the last to start."*

8. Change the **sequence** of that chronic disruption.

> Examples:
>
> *"Next time could you remember to do that hissy fit for about one minute **just before** I pass out the worksheets?"*
>
> *"Could you write your pretend apology statement to little Reginald **in the morning for the things you might say to him during the day?** It will probably save some of your recess time in the afternoon."*
>
> *"Next, your assignment is to go to Time Out for **five minutes before first recess...** and pretend to calm down for something bad that <u>might happen</u> later when you go out on the playground."*
>
> *"Please come to my desk **in the middle of the work period** and give me two pretend excuses for why your homework might not be complete tomorrow."*

9. **Add or subtract** one element from the offensive pattern.

> Examples:
>
> *"Whenever you do your practice 'work avoidance' routine,....**always hold a yellow pencil in your left hand** so I'll know you're on duty."*
>
> *"Each time, **just before** you do one of the pretend excuses, just take your hand and **snap your fingers quietly** (like this). It will help with our communication on this secret assignment."*
>
> *"When you do your morning tattle tales, make your report to me **with one eye closed.**"*

Subtle Transformations:

Steamed and Summarized on the half shell

Here it is boiled down to the basics. If you would like to serve up one of our savory paradoxic requests as a way to get started in the OBM business, do this:

> *1. Encourage the problem behavior,
>   for some good educational reason.*
>
> *2. Take early control of the behavior by
>   requesting a small token change.*
>
> *3. Gradually and methodically erode
>   (or "transform") the behavior
>   through a series of requested
>   shifts in the pattern.*
>
> *4. Absolutely no smirks or chuckling
>   until you reach the safety of
>   your teachers' lounge.*

An Outrageous Look At Reinforcement

Sympathy for Skinner

As you must have gathered by now, we are not real hot on the use of primary tangible reinforcers in our management strategies. On the other hand, some of us have paid our academic dues in the salt mines of applied behavior analysis. I freely confess to being one of those rat-runners and M&M pushers. My personal recovery work does not require bad mouthing the grand old school of behaviorism. We need those folks who are willing to spend a career in the lab with rats and pigeons; cataloging response patterns, cleaning the cages, and developing learning theories. There's no question that classical behavior modification can be effective.

Our concern is not regarding effectiveness, but efficiency. When dealing specifically with oppositional-defiant students, we have found that OBM methods can achieve measurable behavior change in one or two weeks that might otherwise take months of diligent contingency management. For example, by requesting and "reinforcing" *pretend* classroom disruptions, I can quickly extinguish certain disgusting behaviors that might otherwise have required several rolls of happy stickers and weeks of intense teacher effort. Yes, the OBM team may stoop to pushing a few M&M's (or raisins) from time to time, but we are not using them for true operant shaping---just as props in a more sophisticated stratagem.

Secondary Reinforcers Can Still Be Cool

Rather than primary drive reduction through those boring traditional rewards, we get a kick out of some slick social reinforcers. As a tacked on little incentive to insure compliance with our outrageous assignments, we like to grant our students unusual benefits, contrived freedoms, bizarre privileges, outlandish social recognition, and clearly excessive demonstrative praise. These rewards are usually free (*read: no cost to the teacher!*) and are proof that you can often substitute creativity for big bucks. They are also available in the classroom, easily dispensed through coupons or assigned time blocks, and fully under the control of the OBM teacher. Sounds good to me.

The items selected for our *Student Reinforcement Inventory* are only a sampling of the possibilities. We hope the list will bring some grins, but also serve to stimulate some key cell assemblies in your right brain. Hopefully, you will soon be generating many more of your own wild and crazy reinforcers! Brace yourself. <u>This</u> is reinforcement!

Student Reinforcement Inventory

Barry T. Christian, Ph.D. (1997)

_____1. Chewing gum "permit" good for special permission to chew gum for one hour on Friday. Of course the student shouldn't expect the teacher to also supply the gum. He should bring his own ("If you got 'em, chew 'em") or earn the gum separately. The permit bears an authorization signature and must be worn or displayed during the chewing time.

_____2. Sell "time shares" to the reading corner. These are confirmed reservations for special preferred time blocks. As with the real time share racket, you may attach some fine print such as a modest fee for any trading of time blocks.

_____3. Early dismissal to lunch. Hey, even one minute early could mean the difference between indigestion and food tolerance.

_____4. Early dismissal from class or from school. If the local "hit man" bully is after you, a one minute head start can be quite valuable.

_____5. Permission to work quietly on an assignment from another class. Of course this would exclude such things as the term project for Taxidermy Science 101.

_____6. A free admission ticket to the next home game. If the student isn't really into sports, he might scalp the ticket for quick cash.

_____7. Free time to listen to music on a cassette/CD player (with headphones). Bring your own tapes or listen to the teacher's collection of Lawrence Welk favorites.

_____8. Two "free" items on the next Spelling or Math test. Allow the student to circle the two items to be skipped, attach the coupon to the paper, and get full credit for those items.

_____9. Permission to do only alternate items (odd or even numbers) on the homework assignment. The completed half is graded as if it were the entire assignment. _Here's an embedded OBM strategy._ We have found that students who ordinarily resist any homework will complete the truncated assignment---just because they want to use up the coupon. It's kind of like buying a case of cat food that's half-off, even though you don't own a pet.

_____10. Permission to serve as an aide to the teacher, coach, janitor, or a favorite Power Ranger.

_____11. Preferred seating in the classroom: The student uses a coupon as prepaid rent on a favorite desk position in the room. This rental may be for one day, one week, or until there is a disturbance.

_____12. Extra Consultation Coupon: These prepaid coupons are redeemable for special guidance on one difficult work item. Our high self-esteem teachers print up a limited supply of these coupons resembling a $100 bill and displaying their own staff photo instead of good old Ben Franklin. The implicit message to the student is that the teacher's consultation time "don't come cheap" and should be used wisely.

_____13. The privilege of "reserving" a cafeteria table for a select group of friends. Why not block off the table with some of that fancy velvet rope from a movie theater? Maybe even require a black tie for each member of the dinner party.

_____14. While we're at it, how 'bout earning a special reserved seat on the school bus? Better yet, why not earn a prestigious "box seat" at the next school basketball game, drama event, or assembly? Use bright colored crepe paper to designate the VIP seating area.

_____15. Award a "Panic Card" which can be used for urgent care at the Guidance Counselor's office. This card also serves as a hall pass. Let the student know that the Panic Card should be used *before* any crisis gets out of hand (and cannot be used to escape any classroom criminal charges).

_____16. Permission to use the computer to type out responses to the weekly Spelling test. (Note: Be sure the program doesn't have a "spell check" function. You understand the importance of this, right?)

_____17. Opportunity to make an activities announcement over the school's PA system. This announcement may be pre-recorded so the narcissistic student can listen to his own compelling and authoritative voice, (and avoid anxiety!).

_____18. Permission to take part in a very special end-of-year water fight (with buckets, hoses, balloons, or squirt bottles provided). Extra points (roughly six billion) may require the teacher to participate. On the other hand, a teacher armed with a fully charged Super-soaker may find some personal joy facing down the classroom toughguy ("Do you feel lucky, punk?).

_____19. Appointment to serve on a classroom "Kangaroo Kourt" to deliberate appropriate consequences for peer conduct violations arising over the past week.

_____20. The earning of "Auction Bucks" which can be used to bid on a menu of classroom privileges. This auction technique is a good way to measure the relative value of various wacky benefits in the classroom. Don't worry about losing control of a neat privilege. If it's really hot, the bidding will go wild and one crazed obsessive student will sink his entire stash into it.

_____21. Award "Caught-Being-Good" coupons for behavioral and academic achievements. These are signed by the student and proudly deposited in a fish bowl (in the main office) where a broadcasted weekly drawing determines special winners.

_____22. Experiment with the policy of keeping one or more front seats vacant. Whenever a brilliant, or near-genius answer is given, the teacher activates a celebrity music sound track and theatrically announces to the student "come on down!" or "advance to the head of the class!" The selected student then occupies a coveted front seat for the remainder of the class period.

_____23. Witty OBM teachers with unlimited energy might arrange to have "Special Achievement" certificates delivered to students in the form of a singing telegram. Better yet, enlist the principal to be the messenger, dressed in a gorilla outfit or belly dancer costume. (Hey, you won't know until you ask.)

_____24. Begin each classroom day by reading a "Morning Report" patterned after a radio newscast. This should review some noteworthy student achievements from the preceding day (e.g., "Yesterday five students were found to have perfect papers, all student's completed the worksheets, and the teacher smiled three times..."). These reports can get pretty wild, and sound even better if pre-recorded and played back to the class.

Final Delusional Ramblings:

In training workshops I have often suggested the following outrageous procedure: When you get out of your car in the parking lot, look around on the pavement for any piece of worthless scrap you might find (pull tab, squashed pen cap, odd looking pebble, etc.). Bring it in to class and tell bizarre extravagant stories about it all through the day. During the last few minutes of school, test the value now ascribed to that piece of junk by putting it up for class auction. Compare the number of points or credits bid on it with the value paid for earlier items. Sometimes this exercise generates another "pet rock" craze, and of course another millionaire teacher.

True Lies About The Author

Dr. Barry T. Christian is both a clinical psychologist in private practice, and a supervising school psychologist. He has worked in public schools for the past sixteen years performing direct counseling, evaluation, and program development services. Dr. Christian has also provided clinical supervision to many talented Special Education counselors and post-doctoral psychologists. Most of the OBM strategies presented in this book have either come to the author in dreams or been cleverly stolen from classroom teachers and his supervisees.

To make matters worse, this author has presented inservice training workshops to hundreds of unsuspecting teachers and administrators in the Southwest. On many occasions, teachers attempting to implement OBM strategies have disrupted entire school buildings, caused riots and demonstrations among parents, and generated major symptoms of mental disorientation in their difficult students.

Despite these (false) problems, the author continues to present outrageous training workshops for elementary and mid-school faculties. While it is most likely that OBM strategies would never really work with the hard core oppositional-defiant students in your school, you are still welcome to write and request training and resource information.

Barry T. Christian, Ph.D.
School Psychology Services
P.O. Box 5039
Silver City, New Mexico 88062-5039